FREE AND FIRST

UNLOCKING YOUR ULTIMATE LIFE

by Elizabeth Jane

2nd edition

Inspiring Publishers
P.O. Box 159, Calwell, ACT Australia 2905
Email: publishaspg@gmail.com
http://www.inspiringpublishers.com

A catalogue record for this book is available from the National Library of Australia

National Library of Australia The Prepublication Data Service

Author: Elizabeth Jane
Title: Free and First – Unlocking Your Ultimate Life
Genre: Nonfiction

Paperback ISBN: 978-1-923250-04-8
PDF eBook ISBN: 978-1-923250-05-5
ePub2 ISBN: 978-1-923250-06-2

About the Cover

My first painting, *Into the Light,* 2019, graces the front cover of my debut book. The image portrays the human experience of suffering, depicting how we find ourselves in muddy waters, confused and delusional, until our lotus flower finally breaks through into the light and is free to blossom.

Elizabeth Jane acknowledges the Traditional Owners of the lands on which she lives and works and extends her respect to all Aboriginal and Torres Strait Islander peoples throughout Australia. She recognises their continuing connection to land, waters and community and pays her respects to their cultures and knowledge, to the Elders past, present and emerging.

This book is dedicated to those who love me and taught me how to love myself: to my parents, Margie and Russell, who recently celebrated 56 years of marriage, and to my four wonderful, loving children: Jessica, Eliza, Jacqueline and Harrison. Thank you for loving me and for helping me realise the importance of loving myself and putting myself first. May you never forget how amazing and unique you are by being you. I hope that you can always have self-worth to recognise and fully meet your own needs before anyone else's and have the ultimate life.

I love you.

Higher Calling

When will I hear
The symphonies of the birds,
The laughter of children,
The lapping of the sea kissing the shore,
The magical, mysterious sound of silence?

When will I feel
The sunshine on my back,
The wind tousling my hair,
The sea holding me close,
The warmth of sand between my toes,
The softness of a snowflake?

When will I taste the fruit from a tree,
The salt of the sea and of my tears?

When will I smell
The newly cut grass,
The perfume of flowers,
The air after rain?

When will I write the love letter to my heart?
When will I embrace me, embrace humanity?

My child,
When you finally stop
And listen to the incessant calling of your soul.
When you see the majesty of you, of humanity, of all that is
Your beauty, your uniqueness,
You will put yourself first.
It is then that you will see the Miracle of Life unfolding before you,
The Universe supporting your every move toward you.
You are the microcosm of the Universe.
You will have the ultimate life.

Contents

Note-taking page for self-reflection

Introduction

My transformational journey over the past three years has been both challenging and incredibly liberating, as I unveiled my true self. A key to unlocking and freeing myself has been to closely examine my childhood, my parents' roles, my close relationships and my past experiences. Someone once told me, 'everything you need to transform your life for the better is within you.'

I didn't really understand this at the time, but now I do. Our parents, loved ones and past experiences, both good and bad, offer major clues to areas that need healing or releasing. Initially, I told myself, *I am not like my mother. I am an independent woman with a career, and I am the leader of my life!* This was far from the truth because the patterns and programs in my subconscious were quietly and constantly at play.

For this reason, I start this book with a brief description of my life and invite you to reflect on particular traits of your parents–the ones you like and dislike–your relationships with loved ones and your past experiences. Your circumstances, no matter whether you think of them as favourable or not, hold the key to learning about and unlocking the real you. It is only when we are aware and can acknowledge, allow and love all parts of ourselves, that we can truly be free to unlock the ultimate life.

My life pre-transformation

Ever since I was a young child growing up in Melbourne, Australia, I loved to help people. Once I could read, from about the age of six, I would often round up young children in my neighbourhood and play teacher. I am the older of two girls, and my parents raised me as the boy, so to speak. When I was born, the doctor announced, 'you have a beautiful baby girl. What are you going to call her?'

My highly medicated mother replied, 'Andrew James!'

My parents encouraged more stereotypically male-oriented qualities of dominance, responsibility and independence. They pushed me towards more academic and less creative subjects at school. I was an obedient and even-tempered child, qualities that my parents encouraged and admired. By contrast, my younger sister was motivated by my parents to shine her more traditionally female qualities of warmth, caring and sensitivity. She later became a nurse and a homemaker like my mother.

As a young child at my grandparents' farm, which was a three-hour drive west of Melbourne, I remember often lying awake at night, questioning the meaning of life and asking myself, 'why am I here? What is my purpose?' Being in the country gave me a much needed and welcome escape from the inherent pressures of what I thought was expected of me from my family, teachers and friends. It was there that I spent every school holiday. The farm was my companion, and the place where I felt safe as I moved homes and schools five times in my formative years due to my father's work. I would often disappear all day into the paddocks with my grandfather and cousins, with the horses, farm dogs, sheep, cattle and chickens keeping us company. These were fun-filled creative times for me to explore and be free.

Growing up, I excelled at school in academics and sports. In hindsight, I think throwing myself into my studies and sports was my way of distracting myself so as not to confront my needs and feelings. I loved receiving approval, praise and love by impressing my parents and teachers. I had no idea that I could, and needed to, look within myself to meet those needs. Although I had been quite outgoing as a young child, when I started school, I became shy. This was probably a result of all my school moves. I found it easier to keep to myself with only a couple of close friends.

I realise now that my diligence in excelling in studies and sports had become a convenient way of distracting myself from my negative feelings of self-worth. I often felt that I didn't fit in and that I didn't have anything worthwhile to say. Keeping myself busy also ensured that I didn't have to socialise or speak up about how I felt. I was respected by my parents for being even-tempered, so I never allowed myself to show a moody side. I dreaded those lunchtimes when I didn't have organised sports, as I feared that I would have no one to sit with or, worse still, that I would have to share my feelings, which I much preferred to keep to myself. I was petrified that my peers would laugh at me. As a result, I remained quiet most of the time and very rarely gave my opinions or contributed to conversations. I absolutely avoided any public speaking throughout my academic life. In my final year at school, although I fit the mould of a perfect student, becoming a prefect would have been my nightmare, because my preference was to blend in and not draw any attention to myself.

I graduated with a degree in commerce and became a chartered accountant, following in my father's business footsteps and making my parents proud. After all, a business degree was considered a safe option because you could always get a job in bookkeeping. I didn't know what I needed or really what made me happy–except for my time spent on the farm. I didn't allow myself to explore myself more fully. I didn't allow myself to get carried away by my feelings. I now realise that connecting to my emotions is my power because it helps me to fully connect with myself but at the time, I only knew what brought me approval and love from my parents and teachers, so I followed their cues with utmost accuracy.

Right from the start of my career, I was extremely unhappy. It was at this time that I met my future husband. My parents approved of him because he was from a similar socio-economic background. They no doubt saw him capable of maintaining for me the lifestyle I'd been brought up with. Likewise, my in-laws approved of me. With relief, I left my career in chartered accounting and started to follow what brought me joy. I pursued a Diploma in Primary School Education and, after two and a half years of marriage, I started my family, giving birth to four children in the space of five years.

I spent the next twenty years going happily between raising my four children as a stay-at-home mother and competing on the world sailing circuit with my husband. I had learnt to sail very early on in our relationship, because I believed in the old saying that 'couples that play together stay together.' Of course, I also didn't want to miss out on the fun and adventure that sailing brought. At that time, my life was action-packed and bountiful in so many ways and for that, I am extremely thankful.

My healing and transformation

I have always had a strong desire for personal transformation and cared about making a positive difference in the lives and wellbeing of others; however, it was only recently that I began to re-evaluate what was meaningful in my life. In 2017, cracks started to appear in my marriage, and my children had all reached adulthood. I realised that I had somehow lost myself in being a dutiful daughter, wife and mother and that, to make a better life for everyone, I needed to cater for my own needs first. This was a huge revelation for me. Initially, I felt uncomfortable and selfish for putting my needs first because I had been meeting the needs of my parents, teachers, husband and children for so long but once I started allowing my emotions to rise, recognising my needs and putting myself first, my life and the lives of those around me began to transform for the better. I must emphasise that this change took strength, perseverance and courage.

It was a three-year process of healing and transformation, and during this time, I absorbed knowledge and wisdom from a range of spiritual teachers from around the world to seek out my true self. It was an ongoing journey: discovering what I needed, wanted and desired to shape my life. Spirituality has been a godsend–literally! It has raised my consciousness, giving me greater clarity, strength and wisdom to understand the true me and my needs. Even though my life was going pretty well beforehand, it has definitely transformed for the better as a result of this journey. I will emphasise here that the process has not been about a specific religion for me or worshipping a deity, as such. It has been about discovering the God or good within me: my true self or essence.

Having undergone my own transformation, I am now eager to empower others to do the same. I hope to provide tools to ensure that women's true desires and needs are no longer side-lined or ignored, no matter their age or stage of life.

The teachings and practice of Kundalini yoga, combined with the teachings of Sri Sakthi Narayani Amma (Amma for short) and other spiritual teachers, have supported and guided me throughout my transformation. (Please refer to Appendices 3 and 4 at the end of the book for more information on these practices.) All these teachings stress the importance of meditation, mantra and devotional music as a means of opening your heart to access your inner guru or true self's wisdom.

The Indigenous people of Australia also believe in the healing power of Dreamtime chanting which connects us to our true divine selves, the rest of humanity and Mother Earth. By thinking loving and grateful thoughts, as well as following our joy, we each open our heart, and it is then that we are able to connect not only to our higher self (our soul) but also to the infinite universal energy and wisdom that are always there for us. This raises our consciousness (or vibration) to experience a wonderful sense of peace and wellbeing, which is our true essence. The more often we connect to this universal energy, the more we can access and utilise it to develop better health and more wisdom, strength and power. We also become more peaceful and loving towards ourselves and one another, as we start to recognise our connection to all living things and Mother Earth. In essence, individual transformation can lead to a collective transformation of your family, your community and the world.

Living the ultimate life

Do I have the ultimate life? What is the ultimate life? You would likely agree that a life abundant in love, peace, joy, good health, financial security and freedom is a good start. I definitely have all these components today. As you read this book and start adopting the tools it offers, you too will learn to unleash and love the authentic you. And once you show the real you to the world and put yourself first, everyone will love you for you and you will be free to unlock your ultimate life.

You are the only person who can achieve your ultimate life. It is paramount that you find the real you and see yourself as worthy to be yourself and to put yourself first. Embracing anything that fuels your fire and opens your heart is the gateway to self-empowerment.

We are all unique beings, which is something to be celebrated. Once we can step into our authentic selves, life becomes a joyous and adventurous journey. That is not to say that there will not be tumultuous times but that we are better able to ride the waves of life if we can truly see and accept our real and beautiful selves. How many people do you know who can acknowledge themselves and laugh at their mistakes, or forgive themselves and others, and then rectify their mistakes and move on? These abilities are a large focus of this book.

Unfortunately, we box ourselves into who we think we should be and how we think we should act. We conform to the socially accepted norm, and in doing this, we take away our own freedom, often unknowingly. Our birthright is to be happy and free; however, it is only when we put our needs first that we truly free ourselves. Magically, our life then begins to unfold more abundantly.

As my former husband told me recently, I could have taken many trips on my own over our twenty-five years together but I stopped myself. Did I believe that I was not worthy of them? Maybe I thought it was wasteful to spend money on myself while my hard-working husband earned it, or perhaps I thought that our children wouldn't manage or that my husband would miss me? I probably believed all this and more. However, the truth was that I didn't choose to put myself first. I didn't feel or voice my feelings. It was me who refused to turn the key and unlock myself, to travel alone and go when and where I wanted. I didn't believe I deserved it. It takes courage and a great deal of self-love to rise to your full potential.

Recently, I was reading Osho's *The Power of Love: What Does It Take for Love to Last a Lifetime?* His words resonated with me. He writes, '… live your life as an intrinsic value. Do whatsoever you want to do, but don't do it to prove that you are useful. Do it because you love it. Do it because you feel happy doing it. Do it because it is your love, and suddenly everything has a different color and everything becomes luminous.'

Some authors who have influenced me are Dr Wayne Dyer, Dr Kulreet Chaudhary, Nathaniel Branden, Julia Cameron, Pia Mellody and Melody Beattie, among others. I will be referencing them throughout this book, and I encourage you to explore their work more deeply, too.

After my separation from my husband, I realised that it was necessary to explore, get to know and fully accept and love myself. So, I plunged in, dived deep, explored outside my comfort zone, owned up to my own needs and, finally, put myself first. Identifying and accepting who we are, our true nature, takes courage and a good amount of self-worth because we are vulnerable when we expose ourselves. It is so easy to be identified by our egos, consumed by our fears and cut off from our true nature. The old me found it so easy to hide behind a qualification, family members or work, or just to immerse myself in being busy rather than exposing the real me to myself and the wider world.

You have to be brave. It is so easy to stay on the safe, familiar road and miss the opportunity to free yourself and live the life you have always wanted. Today, rather than listening to the negative self-talk within, I choose to listen to my heart.

What If I Told You?

What if I told you
That you chose to come here,
That you chose your parents,
The time of your birth,
For the purpose of shining your light and uplifting the world?
Yes, you!
Would you take the reins of your life?
Put yourself first?

My paintings and poems

My poems and paintings, which you'll find throughout this book, are a direct result of the transformative process I went through. This creative work has been heart-opening for me and has allowed me to express myself and heal. It is also here as a window for you to access and understand my material through your heart as well as your mind. You might also choose to tap into your own creative process. It doesn't have to be painting or poetry, it could be something completely different but equally creative.

The trips I make to India have been influential in my transformational journey and I mention them throughout the book. The moment I returned from one particular trip, I felt a strong desire to paint. My head was saying: *you can't, you have never painted*; *it's a waste of time and money*; *it's quite a ridiculous idea*. But my heart was saying something quite different: *go for it!* I was yearning to pick up a brush. I didn't realise it at the time but this heartfelt decision was similar to when I had left my accounting career to move into primary school teaching. Unlike my head, my heart didn't care about the consequences and whether it worked out, or how much time and money painting would cost, or what people might think. In the end, all the meditation that I had been doing–learning to look inside to what made me happy and free–was what gave me the courage to dive into painting. I am so thankful that I listened to my heart.

I took hold of my first brush in May 2019, when I joined a class of twenty students. To me, as a novice, it looked like they were all busily working on their next masterpiece. I was in awe. There was such flair, such imagination, so many beautiful colours. I'd had no idea what I needed for the class, so my teacher, Cyndi Rogoff, supplied all my brushes, paints and canvas. Cyndi has supported me on my transformational journey. Her studio is in the eastern suburbs of Sydney where she has been teaching for over twenty years. Besides a Bachelor of Fine Arts, she also holds a Master of Art Therapy (refer to Appendix 5 for her website.) Under her direction, I plucked a few photos from the myriad of books that stacked the shelves. All I knew was that I wanted to paint something vivid. I summoned my imagination and let loose my creativity onto the canvas, much as a child would do–without fear.

Into the Light was my first painting. After it came poems and paintings titled, *Moonlight Magic, Let Go* and *Shine Brightly*. The paintings all came in quick succession; most from photographs I had taken around my home in Sydney. Cyndi gave me complete freedom and encouraged me to paint a few simultaneously. I listened to which piece needed me most during each session and lost myself in it.

My poems started to filter in later, mainly in the depths of night. With delight, again like a child, I would stay awake and burrow under the covers, feasting on inspiration and typing words into my phone for safekeeping. Sometimes the images to paint came and other times the poetry emerged.

Before I started writing this book, I kept seeing pelicans. Two, which had been proudly perched on the end of my jetty, were the inspiration for my painting, *Let Go*, and another, which I had seen while I was dining at a waterfront restaurant in Sydney, the night after noticing the first two. I wondered what message this proud bird was trying to impart to me. I was curious and looked up the meaning of this spiritual totem online, at trustedpsychicmediums.com: I learnt that the pelican *symbolises your selflessness and your ability to put other people's needs before yours … you dream about the pelican because you need to change things in your life, so you and your needs come first.* The pelican also symbolises the vital need to let go in order to make room for something better.

I was blown away. And if I needed any more guidance and confirmation, the maître d' had handed me the restaurant's card from that night and it was a postcard with the picture of a pelican! After that, I was sure I was embarking on an adventure of self-discovery.

Free and first

This is a book of firsts for me: my first book, first paintings and first poems. Most importantly, it is about taking the reins of my life for the first time. I feel like a child again: impulsive, joyous and free. It's an incredible feeling, and I know that you can experience it too. Once you do, there is no going back. I believe everyone deserves to be happy, healthy and free and to live their life with purpose.

I encourage you to bookmark or highlight parts you feel relate to you and return to them again and again. Please give a copy to your loved ones too, especially your children. I will share many powerful tools with you, including the *ABCs of me*, *Me Time* and *Meditation*, to assist you on your transformational journey. I believe that these tools apply equally to everyone, particularly women–whether you are a teenager trying to navigate life choices and the future, or a mother balancing so many of life's priorities. Think of it as your workbook to transform yourself, to move up and into your ultimate life.

It's time to take responsibility, to put your needs first, to allow yourself to come into balance and flow, so you too can create the life you deserve. After all, a happier and liberated you is a step in the right direction to a world of peace, love and light. Only a healed you can contribute to healing the world.

With Love,
Elizabeth Jane

Note-taking page for self-reflection

CHAPTER 1

Finding Me

Dreaming

Dreaming

I look outside
And am tossed around
The roller-coaster of life.
Sometimes happy but most of the time in fear, in pain,
Seeing the world through tainted glasses.

When will I have the courage and wisdom to look inside?
To root myself to Mother Earth,
To see Her for real?
I yearn to be called inside so I can awaken,
Disembark from the roller coaster, this picture show of life,
Remember and return to my true essence
And let the real world of loving awareness unravel.

It is Australia Day, 26 January 2019, and I am free for the first time in my life. I feel like I can finally see life for what it is. I am lying by my pool alone when I realise that this is my own life to live as I choose. I am not responsible for anyone but myself. We are all sovereign beings. We enter life alone and leave it alone. I have my own free will to choose what to do and when to do it. For countless Australia Days, I have gone along with things, spending the day not exactly how I would choose but following my family's traditions.

This is the first time in my life I have sat beside my pool alone. *Why did it take me so long?* I ask myself. I have always had a pool but I didn't allow myself that time for me, to choose exactly what I wanted. It was much easier to run around keeping busy, looking after everyone else. It was much more difficult to listen to myself and look after me. Today, it dawned on me that I can be of no real use to anyone else until I look after myself first.

I deeply breathe in the sea air that ripples across my pool and into me like my first breath. I soak up the stillness. How powerful is this revelation? I embrace and love each and every part of me. I have freed myself. I feel like I have transformed into a butterfly. I have shed my old skin that has served me well and am finally free to show my true colours.

True colours

This journey over the last two years has been tumultuous at times but, as I learn to ride the waves, there are definitely more peaks than valleys ahead. As I have started to tap into my emotions and identify my true needs, wants and desires, I am taking the reins on my own life for the first time. Yes, it does take courage but it is also exhilarating! There is much more available to see, enjoy and give. I am much freer being me. Like a butterfly, I have a much better vantage point of the world. As I learn to fly, I am finding that those I love around me are managing to find their wings as well.

If you are ready to be free to shine, to show your true colours, get comfortable, put yourself first and turn the page. I am sure

True Colours

it will take you to an amazing place: back to the true you, where absolutely anything is possible. The sky is limitless. Here comes your ultimate life.

My gap year

I want to take you back in time to the 'gap year' I spent rediscovering myself. As 2018 progresses, I am allowing myself to pursue hobbies and talents that I had put on hold since having my children, who are all now adults. Being separated from my husband, I am no longer piggybacking on his agenda. A new exciting world is opening up, full of amazing, new opportunities.

First, I have travelled alone to India, Thailand and Bali. Exploring these countries and being away from the more privileged bubble of my neighbourhood has helped me gain more perspective on how other people live. Travelling alone has also given me time to feel my emotions without undue distractions. I have had time to reignite my interest in residential property, landscaping and interior design–hobbies I shared with my parents as a child. Expressing myself through design brings me much joy. I have continued my mentoring of young adolescents with Raise Foundation (please refer to Appendix 5 for more information). I have embarked on more mentoring and life coaching courses, as well as training to be a yoga teacher and I have joined the National Art Gallery. My mentoring and these courses have definitely facilitated my transformational journey. Through my creative pursuits, I am rediscovering myself.

As part of this transformation process, I am beginning to realise that I am quietly competent in so many things that I had never allowed myself to own or show to the world. Every time I start to question my self-worth and why my marriage crumbled, I simply give myself more self-love, more Me Time–whether that is through having a massage, yoga or writing this book. This practice of putting myself first is such wonderful therapy. My self-esteem is beginning to recover. I am starting to find me.

I have finally started to let go of past people-pleasing behaviours and habits. I am learning to recognise my needs, wants and desires, and allowing myself to express them. I am allowing space for more balanced, loving and interdependent relationships in the future. As a role model for my children, I am quietly assured that the four of them will live their lives for themselves, putting themselves first. I feel so content and peaceful knowing this. I feel this is one of my greatest achievements.

The lost me

How many women always put themselves first? Not many, I suspect. I definitely hadn't, nor had I ever entertained that question until recently. *So why don't we put ourselves first?* I explored in the following ways.

First holiday for me

How could I reach 52 years of age and never have chosen a holiday purely for me? I asked myself in disbelief. Travelling for my first solo holiday ever, I sat on the plane feeling a quiet sense of anticipation. I felt exhilarated and free thinking about the adventure that was in store– so why had I waited this long?

I had experienced what I thought was a blessed life to date: loving supportive parents, great friends, a loving husband and two careers before having four happy, healthy children who had just reached adulthood. What more could I have wanted?

'My juggle'

I had always juggled my parenting time with partnership time for my husband. I believed this to be the secret potion that would ensure that when the kids all left school, my marriage would be stronger than ever and that he and I could continue to adventure together on our dream life. However, this belief could not have been further from the truth.

'My Juggle,' as I call it, was my choosing not to bother my husband or children with my own needs. I was always fully accommodating my spouse's needs, happily backing onto his hobbies and living wherever his work or play took him. I had no boundaries, a fact I'll explore in the coming chapters. However, I did meet the needs of our beautiful children with better boundaries in place, because when I couldn't meet any of their individual needs, I would always speak up about that.

Little did I know that I was forgetting one vital ingredient: myself. I was so absorbed in my family that it actually never crossed my mind at that time that I wasn't looking after me.

The invisible me

Just before my fifty-second birthday, my husband popped the cork of an aged bottle of wine and announced that he thought we should get a divorce. I was blown away. My amazing world came crashing down around me.

How could this happen? I asked myself. I probably looked forty-five, given that I had always taken care of myself. I had always fully met the needs of my husband and children, so where had I gone wrong? I spiralled into self-doubt and deep feelings of unworthiness.

Finally, after many months of conversations with well-meaning girlfriends and a very expensive psychologist, it struck me: I had forgotten about me. More specifically, after delving deeper, I realised I had chosen not to look at my needs due to my own feelings of unworthiness. As a result, I had slowly become invisible or at best, 'the loving mother,' 'the dutiful personal assistant,' 'the cook,' and my husband no longer saw me for me. I also began to realise that divorce, once the children left school, was a common phenomenon–if not an epidemic–among my peers.

I thought I had cleverly planned my life so our marriage would not dissolve when the kids left school, like so many marriages around me seemed to be doing. I had dutifully taken care of us but not me.

I began to try to understand how I could have lost myself.

Seeking love in all the wrong places

I am interested in whether you can relate to this scenario in my life. I always considered myself the perfect daughter. I always sought to make my parents proud and I achieved that for the most part. As time went on, I sought to please not only my parents but my teachers as well. It was not too long until I was pleasing friends, boyfriends and then finally my husband and four children. How exhausting!

Alongside this people-pleasing trait was a fear of speaking up or having a voice on issues that mattered. I believed this would be counterproductive to keeping everyone happy. Whether it was as simple as giving my opinion on which music I liked or what I really despised doing, I chose most often to keep quiet; to fit in and carry on.

So why had I put everyone ahead of me and not spoken up about my needs, my wants and desires, even as a child? Was it because of conditioning? I now realise that I was seeking love, acceptance and approval from outside myself. I was looking in all the wrong places. If only I had known that love and acceptance had to come from within.

When my marriage began to fall apart, I embarked on my soul-searching gap year, in a similar vein to Elizabeth Gilbert's *Eat, Pray, Love* year. Initially, all I wanted was to escape from the nightmare I was in. I felt unappreciated, unloved and discarded by my husband. Yet rather than looking at these very uncomfortable feelings, I kept my mind and body busy by partying with friends and travelling to parts of Asia and India. It was only when I finally stopped to take a breath from all my busyness and to be alone that I started to find my true self.

When I started to love and accept myself in a meaningful and permanent way, my life and my loved ones' lives began to transform for the better. I spoke up for myself and allowed my repressed anger to empower me by channelling it into setting boundaries and effectively communicating my needs, wants and desires.

At that time, I realised that I could not offer anything to the world until I had healed my core wound of unworthiness. I began to realise this was the reason for my unending people-pleasing: my search to feel needed, accepted and loved.

I went through a roller-coaster of emotions over the following months. First, deep sadness mourning the loss of a life partner, because I had always believed we would be together forever. I spent many weeks crying in the arms of close girlfriends, wondering where I had gone wrong and trying to pin the blame on myself. *If only I had spoken up earlier*, I thought, *then things would be different*.

Some months later, I understood that if I had woken up earlier and allowed myself to meet my needs, it may have resulted in divorce sooner and that could have been to the detriment of our four young children. My husband and I had complemented each other well with our programmed thinking; he provided for the family's security by working long hours and I had provided nurturing and accommodation.

I had always thought I was into marriage equality. However, as I became more self-aware, I realised that I had allowed myself to be second-best, to the disservice of myself as well as my loved ones around me. Although I was very fortunate to have help with housekeeping and children's duties, I failed to realise that I was piggybacking on my husband's adventures, rather than creating my own. I was totally unaware that I was putting my entire family's needs before my own simply because I didn't feel worthy.

Recently, my aunt remarked on hearing of my pending divorce, 'oh, I am so sorry to hear. What will you do now? At least you have grandchildren to look forward to.'

She insinuated that, instead of trying to find myself, I could continue to lose myself by living each day for my offspring's offspring. Is it because of conditioning that mothers tend to lose themselves to those they love? Is it because we are seeking love and acceptance from outside ourselves? Is it because we don't feel worthy to put ourselves first? It is likely a mix of all of these factors, which begin at a young age. Even as a teenager, I had looked for love and approval from my peers, going along with what my friends wanted, even if it was not in my best interests.

Journey to find me

I was too shocked and in the depths of too much sadness to have an immediate comeback to my aunt's question at the time. However, she got me thinking: *how could this happen?* More importantly, how could I unlearn my behaviour and start to put myself first?

I knew I had to start letting go of these behaviours that didn't serve me because I had become unrecognisable even to myself. I knew it would be challenging but I did know one thing about myself: I have always had the focus and determination to grow. All I needed, I thought, was to recognise my worthiness, to be aware of when I was retreating into my old habits of people-pleasing and to have the courage to speak up and break free of those habits. My plan sounded so simple at the time. I couldn't believe it had taken me 52 years to *wake up* to these habits that were creating havoc in my life. I felt a mixture of sadness and anger for falling unknowingly into people-pleasing and over-accommodating behaviours, especially when I realised that these behaviours were not serving me or my loved ones. Unlike my mother and grandmothers, I had thought I was free and an equal to my husband.

At this stage, I was open, and I was completely ready and determined to grow. My journey began to find me.

To Sum Things Up

The 'Lost Me' involved:

- people-pleasing habits;
- looking for love, approval and acceptance from others;
- not speaking up on issues that mattered to me; and
- feeling unworthy and unloved.

Finding Me involved:

- discovering how to put myself first;
- looking for love, approval and acceptance from myself;
- speaking up on issues that mattered and determining what I cared about; and
- embracing the truth that I am worthy, loved and more than enough.

CHAPTER 2

Challenges

Stardust

She pours down from the heavens,
Cleansing, awakening.
Our deep, succulent roots rejoice,
Dancing, untangling,
Planting deeper, exploring farther.
The seed of life bursts,
Surfacing.
Beauty blossoms,
Explosions of colour and scent.
Breathing in the air,
Breathing out,
Breathing no longer,
Returning to stardust.

The ABCs of me

I identified three chronological steps that are crucial to achieving the ultimate life and finding my true self. These 'ABCs of me' are awareness, boundary-setting and communication. A chapter is dedicated to each of these three vital components.

A: ability to be aware, acknowledge, allow and accept my thoughts, emotions and needs.
B: setting clear boundaries.
C: finding the courage to authentically communicate my needs.

Inability to connect to my emotions and express my true needs

As I matured and had children of my own, I became more open, engaging easily with friends and family, as well as total strangers. This attribute has assisted me greatly with my volunteer mentoring because I easily open up and allow mentees to do the same. First, I listen as a compassionate witness to their worries and problems. Then, rather than jumping in with my solutions, I offer to be a sounding board to brainstorm different solutions together as we determine how to meet their needs. Ultimately, the mentees decide on the solution that works best for them.

However, my talent for connecting quickly with others and intuitively understanding their requirements was a paradox, in that I hadn't applied it to myself. I often overlooked my basic need of a supportive husband and father to our children because I didn't feel worthy of identifying and expressing it. Instead, I kept myself busy rescuing or over-accommodating my family and others, which contributed further to the decay of my crumbling marriage. This behaviour was not serving my husband or me.

Rescuing or over-accommodating behaviour

This form of behaviour has a lot to do with a lack of self-worth. If we are busy fully accommodating everyone else, we must be invaluable, right? For me, it had a lot to do with my upbringing and how I saw my parents' roles, which consequently influenced how I saw myself. My parents took on more traditional roles, with my mum being the homemaker while my father 'brought home the bacon.' As I was the firstborn and didn't have a brother, they encouraged me to enter the more male-dominated career of chartered accounting. Also, my qualities of servitude, nurturing and accommodation, although present from an early age, really started to surface more fully when I married and had children of my own.

The truth was that for twenty plus years, I had lost myself in my family of four children and my husband. Until I could first look at myself, my emotions and my needs–and meet them on my own–I could not be there effectively for others and support them on their journey towards a happy, joyful life. I knew I had to find me before I could offer me to the world. As flight attendants remind us, 'in an emergency, please ensure you have secured your own oxygen mask before assisting others.' This is the truth not only for flight emergencies but for our full journey through life.

Self-worth

If we don't have adequate self-worth, we run a very big risk of not recognising or meeting our needs. Without a sense of our self-worth, we get tangled in our self-limiting beliefs and doubts. Numerous books have been written on this topic over the decades. I've learnt a lot from Nathaniel Branden's books, *The Six Pillars of Self-Esteem*, *The Power of Self-Esteem* and *The Psychology of Self-Esteem*. Branden was a leading pioneer in this field. Self-worth starts to blossom only when we learn how to self-love, through allowing ourselves Me Time. The good news is that the benefits can be immediate if we start to love ourselves today. (Feel free to skip to the Me Time chapter and Appendix 2 for self-love practices you can begin implementing.)

Life is a mirror

What I have come to realise is that if you don't truly believe you are worthy of putting yourself first, then no one else will. Life is like a mirror. How you feel about yourself is reflected back at you from those around you, particularly those that are around you most often–your family and close friends. If you don't love and respect yourself, you will probably find that those around you are not loving and respecting you either and will take you for granted. For example, my children would say, 'leave that. Mum will tidy up. She always does.'

For our needs to be authentically communicated and heard, we need to truly believe that we are worthy of having our needs met. If we don't have self-worth, then we steadily spiral into self-denial. This can get messy. We rarely communicate our needs, or if we do, it's not in an authentic, empowered way and others can't hear those needs. Many examples come to mind. My mother never felt deserving of her time being as equal to that of her husband's or children's. She felt she should do, or at least organise, the more menial chores because her family members had more valuable things to do with their time. I thought I was free of this pattern but I often succumbed to over-accommodating everyone before dealing with myself. I found it much easier to fit in with what everyone else wanted, whether that was our dinner menu, television channel or family holiday. Like my mother, I would often deny myself simple personal luxuries even though we could afford them. I didn't feel I could spoil myself. I secretly believed it was a waste to spend time and money on me.

I am more than enough

It is only when we can fully accept who we are, and feel worthy of loving all parts of ourselves, that we can fully recognise our needs, put ourselves first and truly embrace our life. What's stopping you? What are you waiting for?

Accepting who we are takes courage and a good amount of self-worth because exposing ourselves makes us feel vulnerable. It's much easier to hide behind a qualification, family members, work or other things, than to expose our real self to the whole world.

Initially, I found that my thoughts were always heading in the *I am not good enough* or *I am better than* direction. Once I'd started to accept myself, warts and all, I found that I was no longer trying to control, over-accommodate, rescue or seek undue approval from others. I began to free not only myself but my loved ones as well. *I am enough just as I am* became my motto and I began to recognise and love my true self, my needs, my likes and my dislikes. It was only then that I was able set appropriate boundaries and effectively communicate my needs, becoming truly empowered and free.

In the midst of navigating how to set boundaries and accept yourself, there will inevitably be obstacles.

My Rocket Ship

I have boarded my rocket ship.
I have the controls.
The drag is incredible at the start,
Pulling me down into the maya; fear tugs at my tail.
I so want to bring lots of passengers with me
But many have fear.
I must respect their own free will.
I peer through the peephole on life.
It is glistening, magical.
I am free.
The gravitational pull of maya and fear is no longer.
I soar to the heavens.

Good Time Ganesha

Challenges and overcoming them

It was the last month of the COVID-19 lockdown in Sydney when I created *Good Time Ganesha*. My Zoom art class required a teacup and a vase of flowers to be props for a lesson in shading. My heart really did not want to paint a teacup, so I grabbed my statue of Ganesha instead.

Ganesha is an elephant-headed Hindu God and represents the overcoming of obstacles. To call on the energy of Ganesha within you, there is a Sanskrit mantra:

'Om Gam Ganapataye Namaha' (pronounced Om gung gah-nah-pa-tai-yay namaha)

Feel free to try it if you are undertaking a new project or when any problem arises, particularly problems you can see no way through. (Please ensure that you have relaxed with some deep breathing beforehand for maximum effect in calling forth Ganesha's powers.) Hopefully, after chanting, your obstacles will be overcome or reduced and it will then be plain sailing.

No matter what form of obstacle I encounter, I find that the intensity of and ability to overcome the obstacle depend on:

1. My mindset: how I view the issue at hand. Quiet time in meditation gives me greater clarity from a more neutral viewpoint. I can solve the problem more readily, rather than inflame it. (Please refer to Me Time in Chapter 6 for more discussion on meditation.)
2. The action I take: I try to step back from the problem I'm experiencing and ask, *what is the experience trying to show me?*

Over time, I began to recognise my obstacles as opportunities for growth. As I faced the obstacle, by speaking my truth about how I felt, I found that many of the issues resolved themselves. Others around me were also empowered to solve problems of their own as I set and maintained boundaries. When I stopped rescuing my children, they too became more resilient and grew. For example, I no longer assisted so much with homework and structuring their study and playtime. I also ensured their play dates were with other children who they wanted to connect with, rather than the children of mothers I wanted to get to know. Allowing the children to make their own choices didn't always work out favourably for them; however, they learnt what didn't work for them and all chose better options over time.

There are some major obstacles to putting ourselves ahead of others. First, it may be that we can't recognise or aren't aware of our true needs. Second, we may sacrifice our needs with inadequate boundaries, thus giving away our power. Finally, we often don't know how to communicate our needs effectively. In the early days of finding me, all three of those statements applied to me. I wasn't recognising my needs so there was no chance I would be able to communicate them. Also, I was over-accommodating others due to deep feelings of unworthiness, desperately seeking their approval and love. I was certainly in a pickle.

So often we get caught up with looking after what everyone else needs, especially as mothers who are balancing family and work commitments. There is often little opportunity for Me Time. Many of us subconsciously or knowingly try to meet others' approval or expectations, which often means we put our own needs to the side. As a result, we can end up moulding ourselves into who we think we should be and how we think we should act. It's our ego that tries to tell us we have to do something that makes a lot of money or is useful, which leads to people-pleasing behaviours because we outsource our needs and seek approval, love and acceptance outside of ourselves. Often, the ego can override the heartstrings, pulling us away from something we really enjoy. In doing this, we take away our own freedom. It then becomes more difficult to follow our joy.

Challenges that teenaged girls face

Obstacles are not exclusive to adults. As a parent of four children who are now in their early twenties, and as a mentor of children, I see how teenagers are deeply affected by these vital issues of self-worth. Teenagers' most pressing concerns and obstacles are timeless and do not discriminate along socio-economic or racial lines. Certainly, their concerns may come in a slightly different form to the challenges experienced by mothers; however, I believe the common thread between all generations of women is inadequate self-worth or a lack of self-esteem.

What follows is a letter to my teen self, knowing all that I know now. This exercise allowed me to connect more deeply with the challenges faced by my three daughters, and I suggest you do something similar for yourself, regardless of whether or not you have kids.

Dear teenaged Elizabeth,

I know that you race home after school each day to delve deeply into your studies. I get it. You feel safe there and you can distract yourself from those endless *not good enough* thoughts that whir away in your head. You also love making your parents and teachers proud with your top academic and sporting achievements.

Guess what though, a lot of your peers have the same thoughts as you playing over and over in their minds! Instead of trying to mask these thoughts by keeping busy, and trying to get love and approval from their parents like you do, they numb their feelings by drinking, using drugs and having sex, among other distracting risky behaviours. They look to their peers rather than their parents and teachers for approval, acceptance and love.

The best way to get rid of these negative thoughts is by expressing them, acknowledging them and playing detective on why they are persisting. Most of these thoughts are just a sign for you to take more care of yourself and love and support yourself more. These negative thoughts are not necessarily a true reflection of what is happening in your life.

When Harry texted you a few months back to say he couldn't go to the party, because he was sick with appendicitis, you believed that he had found another date; that he had made a mistake asking you.

You felt it was something you'd said to him or maybe it was your fat ankles. You later found out that he truly did have appendicitis but not before you went into overdrive, thinking self-loathing thoughts. Those thoughts emotionally drained you and made you sick and unable to sleep for three days.

Loving yourself *more* than your parents and loving yourself *more* than your best girlfriends as you grow up will give you the strength and courage to stand up to the negative thoughts in your head as well as the bullies in the playground.

I hear you–you love your girlfriends, especially Jane and Kathy who have been by your side now for ten years. That's important as they love and support you for you, and you don't have to pretend around them. They are good for you but I still feel that you need to learn to love yourself more. Once you can do this, life becomes a lot more chilled, and you'll be able to stand up more readily and reject things you don't like. You'll get there eventually, I promise.

At first, you'll feel you are being mean or aggressive when you voice your opinions, and at times it is difficult for you to be assertive because you have been quiet for so long. Remember, it's not the person you need to reject, it's just their particular behaviour that you don't need to accept. I send you so much love as I feel your pain, your fear and your sadness. Fixing this is not something that will happen overnight. It will take practice. No one needs to put up with bullying. Melinda is only picking on you at the moment because she thinks she can. She thinks you are going to stay passive! Don't be hard on yourself, Lizzie.

It's difficult to know how to stand up for yourself. It takes time, courage and perseverance to gain true self-confidence and inner strength. The important thing is to keep practising and not to give up. If you carefully watch some of your friends, they are not there yet either but they are determined to fake it until they make it.

You know the diary that you sometimes write in but usually only the good stuff? Well, start writing about your bad thoughts and feelings to help you process everything. You'll start to feel calmer and stronger in the coming months. Another thing that really helps is doing short meditations and chanting affirmations. At first, you'll protest, saying that you haven't got time, that it's boring and won't help but you'll persevere and surprise yourself at how helpful it is. You'll start feeling good about yourself and this will help to bulletproof you against those that challenge and try to intimidate you.

Regarding your 'fat ankles'–everyone has a part of their physical self that they don't love. The media brainwashes us all to believe that we need to be a certain way, and that to be physically beautiful is the only ticket to happiness and popularity. As your grandma tells you, it *is* what's on the inside that counts. So, start a detox today and cleanse all the negative thoughts, replacing them with affirmations of self-love, such as, *I am unique and enough just as I am.*

I am sure that although it might be a bumpy road for a while, you will learn to accept and love all parts of you, even your wider ankles. This self-love will start to radiate from you, and those around you will start to love you just for being you!

I don't want it to take you until you are 52, so I want to let you in on one final secret. Please stop being so hard on yourself and trying to please everyone. Put yourself first for a change and have some fun! I know that you enjoy stomping in the rain–especially in the gutters on the way home from school–and galloping your horse at the farm. Do more things that bring you joy and allow you to be free to express your true beautiful self.

Sending you so much love,
Elizabeth

What self-jeopardising excuses can you relate to?

Initially, my head or ego was filled with a myriad of reasons why I could not put myself first. It was only when I started to remind myself that these thoughts were my ego trying to keep me in fear and in the poor-little-me mentality, that I made a firm decision not to listen to them. After all, they are just thoughts. Your ego likes to keep you small, sticking to what it thinks is best for you. It also doesn't usually like change, especially change that takes you out of your comfort zone. Your ego is usually not brave; it prefers to adhere to the same safe routine that it knows–even if that's suboptimal for you–rather than take any chances.

Other thoughts that arose for me included: *I thought I was putting myself first*, *I don't deserve to*, *I don't know how to*, *I might get it wrong*, *it's selfish*, *I have children*, *I can't possibly*, *my mother/father never did that*, *I can't spoil myself* and *I have no time or no money for that*. Still other thoughts centred on self-denial: *I prefer to meet everyone's needs before my own*, *I think that I am recognising all my needs and communicating them already*. For a long time, I experienced an underlying fear that if I started to put myself first and voice my opinions, my friends would reject me, my husband might leave me or maybe my children would not love me.

At first, putting my needs first seemed so foreign and selfish to me. This was a huge obstacle to overcome. I realised that I had to work on building my self-worth so I could put myself first and stop thinking I was being selfish. Three years ago, I would have asked myself, *aren't I so much happier looking after everyone else?*

In addition to caring for our four children and my husband, I have also been mentoring teenagers and young single mums on a volunteer basis for eight years. Mentoring brings me so much joy and it has taught me the importance of not rescuing nor over-accommodating. I have now realised that rescuing others was my way of trying to feel worthy but was actually destructive to everyone involved, including me.

For the past twenty-five years, I so efficiently juggled the children and my husband that none of them had to compromise with anything. I was often a so-called 'lawn mower' parent and wife. (See Chapter 4 for more details.) My family's path was always swept and prepped by me. If my husband was busy with work or pursuing his hobbies, then of course I could do the parent and teacher interviews or children's sports carnival without him. I always made sure that clothes were clean, the house tidy and the meals ready. My husband started to gradually drift out of the children's lives but I was always obliging. I did not recognise or communicate my vital need for him to be more fully involved with the children's lives and mine and by the time I did realise, it was too late for him to participate.

Viewing obstacles as opportunities

There are two general categories of obstacles or problems that challenge our wellbeing and prevent us from achieving the ultimate life. They are:

1. Hurdles that need to be overcome to allow us to put ourselves first.
2. Everyday problems that arise.

The wonderful news is that when we start looking closely at the obstacles that prevent us from putting ourselves first, and start speaking up and setting effective boundaries, life's everyday problems tend to diminish. Some problems even dissolve. Albert Einstein said, 'we cannot solve our problems with the same thinking we used when we created them.'

We are always going to be confronted with obstacles in life. However, it's how we view these obstacles that is critical to whether they work for or against us. The old me used to resist problems, rather than welcome and stand back from them and see them as opportunities for growth. Now, I try to surrender to what I cannot change outside of myself. I look to see what I can change within me, by speaking up, standing in my power and setting more effective boundaries. I address the emotional traumas at hand rather than burying them deeper within.

One example of how I shifted my mindset to view an obstacle as an opportunity is the demise of my twenty-five-year marriage. Initially, I had to work through all the emotions that often come with the breakdown of a long-standing relationship, including self-pity, sadness, anger and resentment. However, as time passed, I started to see the marriage breakdown as an opportunity to learn more about myself. What I learnt is that I am responsible for my own happiness. It is up to me to stand up and claim it. The marriage breakup transformed itself into an opportunity to grow and claim my life.

As I started to take responsibility for my needs and ensure adequate boundaries were in effect, the world around me started to become a more peaceful, happier place. Problems started to dissolve completely or at least diminish, because I was standing in my power. I was now at a higher level of thinking or consciousness. As long as I maintained effective boundaries, similar problems stopped occurring altogether.

Another challenge I had to face when my children were very young was debilitating back pain. It was chronic for three years, and then intermittent for another eight. I remember making an appointment for a back operation when I was thirty-three. I told the doctor that I could not function anymore like this; that I had too much pain. I wanted an operation. He simply looked at my scans and said that my back wasn't bad enough for an operation. I was a mess. If I hadn't found hope to continue to step forward, I would have plummeted further with painkillers and antidepressants to mask my pain. Instead, I had focused on another way.

After many trips to specialists, I eventually resolved the pain by allowing my retained emotions to surface and heal. Through my study of Kundalini, I understand that many negative emotions, such as fear, feeling overwhelmed and sadness, are stored in the vertebrae and hips. These restrained emotions can cause us dis-ease, and sometimes develop into disease if they are not acknowledged and expressed.

At the time, I didn't want to listen to how I felt in order to recognise and meet my needs. I had four children under five years old, and I was living in a foreign country, with my husband working incredibly long hours and without friends or family for support. I was fortunate enough to have paid help but I had no one to confide in.

I did not want to acknowledge that the issues in my life were too much to cope with and that I was overloaded. I didn't voice my need for more emotional support, and I felt that no one was there for me. As a result, my back was literally collapsing. If I had spoken up at the time and received more emotional support, I truly believe I would have restored emotional harmony sooner, and it would have alleviated the chronic back pain that had accumulated over many years of my silence. Medication can address the symptoms and be beneficial in times of deep distress or excruciating pain but I believe it often does little to address the cause of the pain to allow it to heal.

For me, this meant my back pain continued over a number of years, even though no injury or physical reason was ever identified by any of my doctors. But once I realised the emotional reasons behind my back pain, it finally left my body for good. Interestingly enough, the pain did flare up again when I was overseas and was told my father was severely unwell and I panicked as I wondered if I could get back home in time but the fear and pain subsided once I was at my father's side.

If I had known twenty years ago, when I first experienced back pain, that I needed to acknowledge, accept and honour the pain as my guardian angel, and to speak up and voice my needs, I could have saved myself a lot of suffering. My back was trying to tell me to care for myself and ask for more support but at the time, I was not willing to listen. I was determined to soldier on and be there for my children and husband. I didn't want to miss out on my young family's adventures or worry any of them with what I was going through. But throughout this painful journey, I had the resilience and optimism I needed.

The virtue of hope is very important when going through massive upheavals and challenges, as it can encourage us to keep moving forward. If we don't realise that the challenges will pass, we can often give up hope.

As I write this from Australia, we are once again in lockdown–like so much of the world–with a resurgence of COVID-19. Hope gives us some comfort that no matter how severe the health and economic ramifications are, this virus will eventually pass. Hope is found deep within us and if we can learn to draw on it, it can give us optimism in the face of adversity. I am the first to admit that hope can be elusive when we have suffered, yet it is the essential light that can free us from our suffering. If I had given up on hope, I probably would not have resolved my back issues or moved on from my failed marriage.

The Miracle of Life

My heart sings
The song of life.
I listen, I hear and I see for the first time.

The wind whispers
The wisdoms of the Universe.
The birds chirp in delight.
The trees sway together,
Dancing, rejoicing.

I turn to the sun.
I breathe in those precious rays.
I am free.
Peace, bliss, love,
Embrace me.

Tools to detangle from self-limiting beliefs

Self-limiting beliefs and programs can be difficult to identify, shift and overcome. Like acquiring any new skill, it requires courage, determination and practice to start undoing restrictive, self-defeating habits and to start to put yourself first. There may be times, as I experienced, when you find yourself reverting to looking after everyone else before yourself. Please don't judge yourself; just give yourself more love, implement the tools outlined below and carry on.

1. Break goals down into smaller, achievable steps. Reassure yourself and reward yourself when you make baby steps forward. For example, simply giving my opinion when it contrasted with another's, or stating that I didn't feel like doing something that was expected of me, was a step in the right direction of listening to how I felt.
2. Don't self-sabotage. There is no point in judging yourself when you make an occasional backward step. Practise self-love and self-care. Remember that you are learning what you do and don't like. Reassure yourself that you are experimenting, trying to set boundaries and that it is definitely better than continuing with no boundaries at all.
3. Only do the things you have to do. When you find yourself constantly thinking negative thoughts and are feeling overwhelmed, try replacing that negativity with thoughts such as, *I am only going to do the things right now that I have to do, and give myself some well needed Me Time.*
4. Remind yourself that it's what you learn along the way rather than the end result that is more satisfying and can bring much happiness. Enjoy the journey. Like a climber, enjoy the view when you reach each higher level, not just the mountaintop. Your ultimate life may not happen overnight.

5. Seek out support. Let's be clear about what type of support I am suggesting. If you are going through an acrimonious divorce or just lost your job, I am not talking about ringing friends to inflame the drama. Vengeful acts and anger only lead to you feeling worse. It is now that you have to summon all your courage and consider the challenge ahead carefully. Create a game plan: call a caring friend, a therapist or a family member who is kind and has good boundaries. This is not the time for self-pity and self-loathing. You need to play your cards carefully and strategically. For example, when my divorce became more challenging, I immediately shared the load with three legal friends, and together we created an immediate game plan. This helped me to stay in my power and to feel proactive, rather than spiralling down into the depths of despair and self-pity. As my grandmother often told me, 'a problem shared is a problem halved.' My three chosen friends were perfect for strategic and emotional support. I also meditated on the issues. This allowed me to look more objectively at my challenges or obstacles. Over time, I found that many challenges resolved and became more of an opportunity to stand in my power.

My setbacks

Initially, there were many setbacks to putting myself first and these actions all had one thing in common: they all numbed my pain. My setbacks included overwork and staying overly busy; excessive exposure to negative news; spending time with negative, low-energy people; over-accommodating others; overly focusing on my children and husband; not saying no and indulging in excessive screen time.

Frequently, I would find myself working until I was physically and emotionally exhausted. I would adopt the often subconscious mentality that I was not worthy if I wasn't staying busy. I would find myself partying hard, which did not leave me in a good place. My visits down to the pub to drown my sorrows and immerse myself in endless judgemental gossip, also did nothing to raise my 'feel-good vibes.' Engaging in excessive listening to negative news also made me feel worse. This had the effect of closing my heart rather than opening it.

Consider which of the above-mentioned self-jeopardising thoughts could apply to you and then highlight them or make a list of your own self-jeopardising thoughts. To deal with self-jeopardising thoughts, we need to focus on and invest in ourselves. (See Chapter 6 for more on this topic.)

In hindsight, all of my setbacks were the result of me not wanting to look at myself, how I was feeling or what I needed. They were all convenient ways of numbing out and not listening to my emotions. As my self-worth spiralled downward, I began to judge myself, which led to more downward spiralling. Gradually, I learnt that the only way upwards and out of the mess I was in was to forgive myself, shower myself in love, reinforce and reactivate my boundaries, invest in Me Time and follow my joy.

To Sum Things Up

The ABCs of me:

- acknowledge and accept emotions to identify needs;
- boundaries need to be established and communicated for needs to be met;
- inadequate self-worth can result in needs not being recognised or met;
- life is a mirror: what you reflect is what you receive; and
- Me Time develops self-worth.

Challenges and overcoming them:

- engaging in activities that numb the pain is counterproductive to solving the problems or obstacles;
- when you experience setbacks, self-forgiveness and self-love (including Me Time) are essential to being able to move into a better space where problems can be viewed more neutrally; and
- when a problem is seen as an opportunity to grow and the issue is faced by speaking your truth about how you feel, the problem often diminishes or disappears completely.

Note-taking page for self-reflection

CHAPTER 3

Acknowledging, Allowing and Accepting

Moonlight Magic

Acknowledging, allowing and accepting our thoughts, emotions and needs is vital for maintaining a healthy sense of self and wellbeing. We are then in a position to recognise our needs. This is the first step in the ABCs of me.

Acknowledging

'We think too much and feel too little,' said Charlie Chaplin.

In this busy, action-packed world we inhabit, most people don't find time to stop and recognise what they are feeling. Our society also doesn't encourage us to express our emotions.

Most people tend to go about their lives containing and restraining their emotions. They are much more likely to welcome and share positive, prettier emotions, such as happiness, joy, bliss, peace and contentment, rather than their 'uglier' counterparts of grief, anger, resentment and fear. We get proficient at containing these emotions.

Many of us have been brought up to believe that we need to be brave when facing adversity and that to show our true feelings is a sign of weakness, whereas I believe the opposite is true. It most often requires great courage to express vulnerability. To sit with your feelings and acknowledge, allow and accept them is the first vital step towards connecting with the authentic you. It is only then that you can begin to recognise and free yourself from limiting patterns, behaviours and programming.

When we don't acknowledge our emotions, it can seriously impact our physical wellbeing. Initially, these contained emotions may be experienced as tight shoulders or a stiff neck, and that is something the majority of us have felt. If emotions are not expressed and are allowed to build up within us over the years, this can have health ramifications, initially in the form of dis-ease and later, disease.

Whether we are feeling positive or negative emotions depends heavily on our thoughts at the time of those emotions. If we acknowledge our emotions, we can observe our thoughts more easily, and we are then in a position to choose whether or not our thoughts are worth being spoken aloud or acted upon. We can also more readily identify our needs and whether they are being met.

To feel and acknowledge our emotions, we need to slow down and actually stop. Like so many, I have become very proficient at keeping busy so as not to feel the unpopular, ugly emotions of anger, sadness, depression and fear. I vividly remember an early Kundalini class when, during the meditative section it suddenly all became too much. Unable to bear it, I picked up my shoes and ran barefoot back to the safety of my car where I sat and cried for a good half hour. After that, I felt a lot calmer and lighter.

My second painting, *Moonlight Magic*, was created from my bedroom overlooking Sydney Harbour, during some contemplative Me Time. After its completion, I found a piece of driftwood while swimming next to my home. It followed the lines of my painted tree so accurately that I attached it to the painting.

Acknowledging your emotions can be as simple as announcing to yourself how you feel in any one moment. For example, *I feel absolutely rotten right now* or *I feel sad, depressed and so much grief that I feel a fountain of tears could engulf me at any moment.* Journaling is another good way of allowing your emotions to be acknowledged and expressed, and so is taking up a creative hobby such as playing an instrument, painting or taking a cooking or dance class.

As we acknowledge our emotions, we begin to deal more with our thoughts. If we are feeling good, we are probably thinking good thoughts, and the opposite if we're feeling bad. According to the National Science Foundation, we have up to 60,000 thoughts per day. Unfortunately, up to 80 percent of these thoughts are negative and revolve around not putting ourselves first. In addition, up to 95 percent of these repetitive thoughts, recycled day after day, are about the past or the future and have nothing to do with the present.

The more negative our thoughts are, the more we are emotionally and physically drained by them. Thankfully, we don't consciously experience 60,000 emotions or feelings per day but how we are feeling at the time can alert us to whether we are thinking good or bad thoughts. We can decide not to be led by the negative thoughts in our head that want to keep us small, angry or sad, and instead choose to follow our heart. Here are three techniques to de-emphasise negative thoughts and return to a sense of wellbeing that I have found success with:

The surrender clap

This technique involves gifting the negative thoughts to the Universe to be transmuted into love and light before they are turned into actions or words. The steps are as follows:

1. Clap your hands together three times, then scrape an open palm upwards for the Universe, consciously thinking, *please Universe, take care.*
2. Forgive yourself for thinking the negative thought (shame only makes you feel worse).
3. Replace the negative thought with one that is more positive and useful.

Naughty children on the school bus

This technique involves imagining a school bus filled with children. The good children get to sit at the front of the bus and the naughty ones at the back, with seatbelts to keep them in place. The good children in this analogy are courage, strength, love, peace, worthiness, etc., and they make the journey of life a lot more pleasant. While the bad children, like fear, anger, misery, etc., are distracting and make the journey a struggle, so securing them towards the rear of the bus stops them from influencing you as you navigate life. Using this technique allows the negative thoughts and emotions to be acknowledged but de-emphasised.

Grey clouds always pass

This technique involves acknowledging the emotion and the thoughts behind it and slowly breathing the emotion out instead of attaching to it. Realise that any emotion you are experiencing will pass once you have acknowledged, allowed and accepted the negative thoughts. Being attached to thoughts, talking about them over and over again, just gives them more energy. You can think about breathing in loving thoughts and breathing out fearful or angry thoughts, or just about releasing the stresses of the day, if this helps. After all, the sky is always blue but sometimes clouds move across it.

(The second and third of these were given to me by two of my favourite teachers, Antoinette Sampson and Jenny Nurick. Please refer to Appendix 5 for their website details.)

The COVID-19 pandemic and de-emphasising fear

At the time of writing, in April and May of 2020, the world is in the grips of the COVID-19 pandemic. We are justified in feeling fearful as many lives and livelihoods have been adversely impacted. However, if we focus on our fear, it can consume us and plunge us further into more despair and negativity. Alternatively, we can unite and take time to reflect on what we can learn from this pandemic. It's an opportunity to spring clean our lives; to look within to see what's working and what isn't. Let's simply focus on what's working and how to have more of it. How can we create a better world together, and be more connected to one another and the planet than ever before? I feel this epidemic is an opportunity to give birth to a higher consciousness, where we can rise together with open hearts, away from low vibrational fear and separation and into more creativity, connection, freedom and love.

Allowing

When our negative thoughts can't be de-emphasised using the above techniques, the best option is to allow the emotions that result to be expressed in a safe place. Over the past three years, my Kundalini yoga classes have afforded me a place to experience and express my emotions freely, and I often find tears welling up or get other sensations in my body which require a safe place for me to experience them. You might try a similar practice or create a safe space in your home where you can express your emotions. If private time can be set aside regularly to do this, you will feel a lot lighter as you allow the emotions to move through you.

Acceptance

We have acknowledged and allowed our emotions–the final step is acceptance. Accepting our more negative emotions can be difficult for most people. After all, no one likes to think of themselves as morbidly depressed, resentful, angry or fearful. However, these negative emotions are best accepted and even welcomed, just as much as their more positive counterparts. They are actually our warning mechanism and our guardian angels, coming to tell us that something is not right. They will continue to tap us on our shoulder until we address the issue at hand and take corrective action. I'll explain this more in the next chapter.

Once we can acknowledge, allow and accept our emotions, they are able to pass through us and are no longer restrained within us. We immediately feel a sense of relief. We feel lighter and unburdened. It is only when we have truly accepted our emotions that we can start to recognise our needs, and to acknowledge what we do and don't want in our lives. We will then give ourselves the opportunity to speak up and put our needs first.

As we put our own needs first, we begin to understand our inner child. This idea has been written about by many authors, including Dr Charles Whitfield in his book *Healing the Child Within*. Our inner child needs are simply our emotional core needs that must be met for us to optimally function. As babies, we need to be fed, watered, loved and kept safe to flourish. As we grow, we also require respect, approval, acceptance, fun, security, sleep and solitude. One method of re-parenting the inner child in therapy was originated by art therapist Lucia Capacchione in 1976 and documented in her book, *Recovery of Your Inner Child.* Julia Cameron also writes extensively on this topic in her book, *The Artist's Way.*

Essentially, to feel good about ourselves, we need to look within and recognise when our basic needs are not being met. It is important to remember that once we become adults, it is no one else's responsibility to meet these needs. We must meet our own needs to survive but, more importantly, to allow ourselves to flourish and be free.

To Sum Things Up

- our thoughts dictate our emotions;
- acknowledging, allowing and accepting our thoughts and emotions will mean that they are no longer contained and restrained within us;
- acknowledging our emotions helps us recognise our needs;
- by de-emphasising negative thoughts, we can return to a sense of wellbeing; and
- we must meet our emotional core needs ourselves, to survive, thrive and be free.

CHAPTER 4

Boundaries

Untamed

Once you have identified all your ultimate wants and needs, boundaries are necessary to ensure that they are met. Boundaries should define what you are comfortable with and how you like to be treated by others. They ensure that you can feel safe, happy and free in all areas of your life. Boundaries should be clear, specific, direct and neither too loose nor too rigid. They may need to be adjusted several times a year as your life unfolds.

Healthy boundaries include everything from speaking up when you think you are being disrespected to having time for your own interests. Many books have been written on the topic of boundaries. I recommend Cristien Storm's *Empowered Boundaries* and Nathaniel Branden's *Six Pillars of Self-Esteem*, should you wish to explore this subject matter further. It is relatively easy to see when a friend has a problem with boundaries but it is often very difficult to see when we have the problem ourselves. This fact became very evident to me when I continued happily running errands for my husband after he had popped the cork announcing that he thought it best for us to divorce! If we lack boundaries, or they are inadequate, then we are overlooking our needs and are far from putting ourselves first.

What dissolved my twenty-five-year marriage? I have pondered this question over and over in my head. I believe it was inadequate boundaries: over-accommodating, not speaking up about how I felt, saying yes to things when I really meant no. The problem was that most of the time I found it difficult to identify my own missing or inadequate boundaries. This was especially problematic for me because I was not in the habit of acknowledging my emotions and therefore my needs. A tool to address this problem is discussed below and was given to me by my valued friend, Valerie Norton, a Family Dispute Resolution Practitioner who cofounded Collaborative Mediation Practice.

Boundaries are usually not in place, or have been overstepped when:

1. You find yourself giving away your power.
2. You are in a co-dependent relationship.
3. You say yes to things that are not in your best interests.

Here is a little more detail about each of these steps.

1. You find yourself giving away your power.

Giving your power away is giving it to others but doing it conditionally and expecting something in return. It involves sacrificing your needs. When you give your power away to others, boundaries are not in place or are inadequate. Many of us spend a great proportion of our lives doing things, trying to be useful and seeking approval and acceptance from others. This can be emotionally draining. However, once we learn to accept ourselves as we are–that we are enough–we begin to feel worthy and thus comfortable setting boundaries. It is then we are free to follow what we love, and meet our own needs before those of others. We can start to retain our power; to love, accept and approve of ourselves rather than looking to others to give us these core needs.

I have mentioned this previously but I mention it again because it is so powerful. Osho, in his book *The Power of Love,* wrote, 'we have been conditioned to be of some utility … you are enough as you are. I am saying to live your life as an intrinsic value. Do whatsoever you want to do, but don't do it to prove that you are useful. Do it because you love it. Do it because you feel happy doing it. Do it because it is your love, and suddenly everything has a different color and everything becomes luminous.'

2. You are in a co-dependent relationship.

I define a co-dependent relationship simply as a relationship where one person depends or relies excessively on another for their needs to be met, such as relying on another for approval, love or a sense of identity. Melody Beattie and Pia Mellody are experts in this field. (For further reading, please refer to Appendix 4.)

If we have effective boundaries in place, we can successfully move from co-dependence to interdependence. We free not only ourselves but also others to whom we are connected. It's a win-win situation as everyone can step into their power and be free to be who they want to be.

How exactly do we move away from co-dependence? First, we need to start meeting our core needs ourselves. When we enter a relationship, it is important that we don't sacrifice our needs. We need to step back and identify what makes us happy and what doesn't within this new relationship.

Healthy boundaries allow you to be yourself while still embracing your loved one. You don't need to reject your loved one, just the specific thing or behaviour that bothers you. Refusing to set good boundaries and not explaining your discomfort does not protect the relationship. This type of behaviour builds walls in the relationship because feelings and needs are not adequately communicated. Over time, intimacy starts to fade when you are not sharing the true you with your partner. Our loved ones have just as much to gain if we meet our needs first, because it frees them from us having control over their life. For instance, I always tended to sugar-coat situations with my family as I thought I was keeping a harmonised, happy, home environment by fully accommodating everyone but would end up being overwhelmed. I now realise that it would have been better to enforce effective boundaries by telling them how I was feeling and what I could and couldn't do. This would have allowed my children and husband to be faced with the truth of the situation. They could then have stepped into their power, and we could have addressed the problems together as a team.

Rescuing behaviour creates co-dependence and is counterproductive, because it keeps everyone captive and unable to assert themselves regarding their needs, and unable to be free. It is disempowering for all involved and, left unattended, it ultimately dissolves connection and intimacy. Thankfully, with a large family, my accommodating was not as extensive as it could have been and it allowed the children certain freedoms as they developed.

3. You say yes to things that are not in your best interests.

Setting effective boundaries can be as easy as learning to say 'no' to uninspiring, self-limiting choices and saying 'yes' to liberating, self-empowering ones. Listen to what you need and follow your joy. Many of us lose track of how we feel and don't exercise our free will to take care of our needs. When I started to listen to my needs and respect myself, my time and my space, my loved ones started to respect me as well. It was that simple. When I stopped saying 'yes' when I meant 'no,' my life started to change for the better.

At first, this new behaviour felt extremely uncomfortable. I felt I was being uncaring and selfish. For example, a very new friend recently visited me and stayed at my house for a month. I had been happy for him to stay for a week but I failed to speak up and tell him. When I finally gained the courage to express how I felt and what I needed–for him to leave–I felt a heavy weight lift off me.

Similarly, during the recent COVID-19 pandemic, there were times when I had seven children in their twenties (my four children plus their partners) working from my home. I love them all dearly but I felt overwhelmed as every space had become their space. My home began to resemble a youth hostel, with offices set up in different areas of the house and bedrooms all in disarray. Mindful of my boundaries, I spoke up and my house returned to normal, with everyone respecting my space and my needs. I felt a welcome sense of relief and a return to well-being.

Boundaries and emotions

A wonderful American Kundalini master, GuruMeher Khalsa, with whom I completed a workshop recently, discusses using your emotions as very positive guides to get you out of trouble and into peace and happiness. I believe that our negative emotions can be seen as our guardian angels, or superheroes, as GuruMeher refers to them in his book, *Senses of the Soul.* Our emotions warn us when something is not right, that a boundary is not in place or is being overstepped. Let's look at three of our guardian angel emotions:

Guardian Angel Anger

When you experience anger, you have three choices:

1. Do nothing. Keep busy or numb that feeling, containing the emotion within.
2. Allow the volcano to erupt.
3. Channel the emotion into something productive or positive that works for you and that makes you feel better about yourself.

I know it does appear obvious that the third alternative is best but it tends to be the least chosen. Anger is showing up to alert you that something is not right, that you are not feeling good about a person or situation you are in. It may mean that someone has taken or is trying to take your power away. By speaking up, saying how we feel and setting a boundary so that this behaviour doesn't continue, we can channel the anger more effectively.

Guardian Angel Grief or Depression

Often hidden, grief and depression also alert us to set a boundary so we can start to feel good again. If grief has been buried within and not been looked at for some time, it may have developed into depression. Once we have acknowledged, allowed and accepted these emotions, we likely need a boundary that involves more self-love. If we just want to cry in bed with the blanket pulled up over our head or we choose to demolish the ice cream tub, then that is what we are going to do. It is important not to feel guilty or ashamed of what we need to initially do to feel better. But as we start to feel better, we will be better able to choose more nurturing and nourishing alternatives. The moment we choose to put ourselves first, we start to free and heal ourselves. (Please refer to Chapter 6, Me Time, for more on these practices.)

Guardian Angel Fear

When we find ourselves seeking approval or wanting to control something, we are often in fear. We are in our head or ego and not in our heart, and our Guardian Angel Fear is alerting us that we need to take measures to feel secure and safe. At this unprecedented time during the COVID-19 pandemic, if we are in fear, we will be resistant to changing our own patterns and behaviour. We want life to go back to what it was like. However, if we can feel safe, we can walk towards the fear and look proactively at this time as an opportunity to take stock of what's working and what's not. In order to feel safe, we need to be able to experience and voice our fears and concerns; to be heard and witnessed without judgement; to creatively express our fear so it may be released.

Expressing our fear may be as simple as talking to a trusted friend or counsellor. Maybe it is pursuing some creative hobby, like journal writing, painting, singing or dancing. Anything that will allow us to acknowledge, express and process the fear in a safe, held environment will be helpful. As I painted *Untamed,* I was able to channel the emotions of sadness, fear and anger that I was experiencing at that time. I threw down various combined paints and mixed them with a modelling compound onto a six-foot-tall canvas using a spatula rather than a paint brush. It doesn't matter what kind of process you choose. (I only started modelling clay for the first time last week.)

Adopting any creative activity that you are drawn to is an opportunity to reflect and put into action steps to heal ourselves, our loved ones, the broader community and Mother Nature by moving away from fear into creativity, connectivity and love. Once we can face our fears, we are free.

Boundaries and your children

Not putting yourself first can be more harmful to your children than you realise–often what we call both 'helicopter' and 'lawn mower' parenting. Watch out if you tend to be the first–a controlling parent who hovers over your children and are overly involved in their lives–or the second, the kind of parent who mows down obstacles before their kids even reach them. Even though they mean well, these parents can hurt more than help their children. Such relationships between parent and child are co-dependent and healthy boundaries are not in place.

Disadvantages of helicopter and lawnmower parenting are discussed by Amy Morin, a leading international psychotherapist, in her book, *13 Things Mentally Strong People Don't Do*. Studies show that children in these situations are less resilient, don't learn to problem-solve as effectively, or to advocate or speak up for themselves. In addition, these children often have less confidence because they start to believe that they can't do things on their own. Controlling parents often foster poor mental health. They calm their kids when they're upset, cheer them up when they're sad and entertain them when they are bored but by taking full responsibility for these emotions, these parents stop their children from learning to regulate their own feelings, which is detrimental to their mental health. If children can't recognise and accept their emotions, they cannot recognise and meet their own needs.

We are our children's first and most important teachers and role models. Our children need to see us being aware of and expressing our needs so they learn to do the same, especially if they later choose to be parents themselves. This awareness and expression allow growth and liberation for all.

When I was sixteen years old, I decided that if I was to have children–and I could afford to–I would have four. It was a huge statement but I think my intuition was guiding me that to have any less, with my perfectionist, controlling nature, I would stifle their development. In short, I think I would have fallen squarely into the helicopter or lawn mower category of parenting myself.

By having four children, I had time to guide but not hover over their lives. I encouraged them to explore life and define what they needed. During their middle school years, three of my children decided to go to boarding school for a year or more, and my youngest decided to change to a more relaxed state school to 'learn more about life.' These experiences allowed the kids to have breathing space, wherein they were left to face their own challenges. They all grew incredibly as a result, learning about what worked and what didn't work for them.

Yet, it was a bumpy road for a while regarding my youngest's decision to change schools. Many of my well-meaning friends thought I was crazy and judged me for what they saw to be a relaxing of my parental duties. I think they believed I was putting my youngest into harm's way. It took courage and a certain amount of faith but in retrospect, relaxing my control was the best thing I could have done as a parent. I certainly had a frank chat about my fears and concerns with my youngest prior to her change of school. I was worried that her grades would drop, that she would get into the wrong peer group or even that her school change would not look good on her CV when pursuing a career later on. How silly these fears appear when I look back.

I feel that personal growth rather than purely academic growth was a good focus for these often seen as troublesome teenage years. Allowing the kids to see my vulnerability and to tread their own path allowed them to develop into the resilient, balanced and independent adults they are today. Stepping back from my kids in these crucial school years allowed them all to step up.

I was fortunate that my husband supported my parenting style. The kids each had the space they needed to find themselves. I am very thankful that I had the foresight and was able to allow them to follow what they felt they needed in order to grow and flourish. Like most parents, mine wanted only the best for me and my younger sister but they often smoothed over bumps in the road. I think it's an ingrained mechanism for a mother to want to protect her children from difficulties. Personally, I feel that it's great if you can allow your children more freedom as they develop, while sharing your fears and concerns with them along the way. It fosters understanding and connectivity. I am certainly not saying that what worked for my family will necessarily work for yours. It is a personal family decision and dependent on the character and developmental stages of your children.

I invite you to discuss your fears and concerns about extending freedom with your children. I found that this was a dynamic process and was dependent on where the kids' physical and emotional development were at the time. You may also find that your children will open up and share their concerns and fears through this process. I definitely feel this freer method of parenting brought the children and me much closer, because we developed a good level of trust and respect for one another. They also learnt to advocate for themselves from an early age as to how much freedom they felt they needed.

I was, however, sometimes guilty of helicoptering and lawn mowing. Some examples included finishing overdue assignments while they slept, tidying their rooms while they were at school and taking over pet duties that had been neglected by them. I accept that my behaviour in those instances may have curbed their problem-solving and organisational skills to a certain degree. In addition, I would often drive them to school when they were perfectly capable of catching public transport–but I balanced this with the enjoyment of these commutes and how I would find out more about their social lives and how they were feeling.

Maybe some readers can relate to this or similar behaviour but I say again, if we are heavily hovering or mowing down our children's obstacles, we are doing ourselves and our children a huge disservice. Their obstacles are their opportunities to grow. We all learn much more through experiencing failure. I learnt through the process of my divorce that when I sugar-coated and controlled my family's life, I was confining us all. We were not free to grow and uncover our amazing selves.

Boundary-setting

Setting boundaries, especially when you are not used to it, can be difficult and uncomfortable at first. It requires courage and takes practice. It is important that you are not too hard on yourself if you first don't succeed. Judgement is the opposite to self-love.

As I became aware of my needs, I realised that there were certain areas of my life where boundaries were missing or inadequate. I'm grateful to my girlfriend, Valerie, who taught me a valuable tool, which I have called the Boundary Self-Check Test. (I mentioned Valerie earlier; she is a co-founder of Collaborative Mediation Practice in Sydney.) This test has greatly assisted me in establishing and maintaining boundaries.

Boundary Self-Check Test

This test can be implemented anytime and anywhere. It is a foolproof way of detecting whether or not you are meeting your needs and have adequate boundaries in place:

1. Think of your loved one's request to you.
2. Rephrase the request as though you were asking it of your loved one.
3. How do you feel?
4. Is it a reasonable request?

Quite simply, if you don't find the request reasonable, accepting it means you are not meeting your own needs. Chances are, you will be overstepping your boundaries and giving away your power.

To Sum Things Up

- boundaries are necessary to ensure that your needs are being met;
- your negative emotions are your guardian angels, alerting you that your needs are not being met;
- inadequate boundaries can lead to co-dependency, where you are disempowering yourself and others; and
- the Self-Check Test helps ensure that you are implementing and enforcing appropriate boundaries.

Note-taking page for self-reflection

CHAPTER 5

Communication of Boundaries

Assume for a moment that we are acquainted with our emotional self and can recognise our needs. (Feel free to return to the previous two chapters if you need a refresher on what the ABCs of me entail.) The final step to improvement is to authentically communicate our needs to establish and maintain effective boundaries.

To express or communicate our needs in an effective, empowered manner is not something that comes easily to most people; however, it is vital for our wellbeing. Empowered communication is an acquired skill. Like any new skill, I believe you need courage, practice and determination to perfect it.

I was recently blessed to spend an afternoon with a friend's family of peacocks at their farm in Byron Bay. I was immediately drawn to a male with his magnificent, coloured plumage, who noisily tried to join us at the outdoor dining table laughing like a kookaburra–he was definitely not shy. Besides being so majestic, bold and graceful, peacocks are also clearly very good mimics of sound, and must have extremely refined listening skills to be able to imitate so accurately. I remember that as evening approached, each of the four peacocks–two male and two female–flew into their own tree to sleep for the night.

I mention this because, to me, these graceful birds symbolise finding an authentic voice, having the courage to sing your own song and being able to listen intently to the songs of others, without judgement. Peacocks also remind us not to take life too seriously but to be able to boldly laugh at what life sometimes offers us. I couldn't resist painting this majestic bird because it embodies the qualities I hope to convey.

For communication to be effective and empowering, it must be responsive rather than reactive; authentic, heartfelt and assertive (rather than passive or aggressive), and two-way.

I was fortunate to have two of my wonderful teachers, Antoinette and Jenny, share tools and techniques with me during their informative and hands-on workshops which helped to strengthen my communication capabilities.

Communicating from the heart

To respond rather than react can be very challenging initially. It takes both focus and practice. However, over time, I started to stand back and not immediately react to a request or comment. I allowed space to consider whether it was my monkey mind (like the ego) and my internal issues that were clouding my judgement. This technique is a skill that I have acquired from my meditation discipline, which will be discussed in the upcoming chapter. Once I had some clarity, I could respond rather than react. Sometimes a few deep breaths or counting to ten under my breath was sufficient. At other times, a longer period was required to neutralise what had been said. And there were occasions when I responded in a manner to buy myself more time. I might have said, 'I hear what you are saying. Can I have until tomorrow to think through what you have told me before I come back to you?'

Initially, communicating authentically was really difficult. I soon realised that I had to both understand my needs clearly and believe that I was worthy to have those needs met, before I could be properly heard. But, unlike the peacock, I realised it was no good mimicking another's cries; it had to be my voice and what I genuinely needed to say. To be assertive, I had to find my voice, which took practice and courage. At first, I felt my assertive behaviour was aggressive, having been passive for so long in suppressing my needs but after a lot of experimenting–going from passive to the other extreme of aggressive communication–I began to find a voice that was assertive. It definitely took some time to gain this balance, and I tried not to be disheartened at those times when I failed to communicate in an empowered way.

Stepping Out

I also tried to be in my heart and not in my head when communicating, to ensure again that I didn't come across as aggressive. I mainly achieved this by putting myself in the other person's shoes and listening intently, like the peacock, to gauge how the other person was feeling and what they were really saying or wanting. I soon realised that my heart-centred approach was very powerful and enhanced both our connection and my understanding.

Communication is a two-way street

For empowered communication, we cannot overlook the other party in the conversation. It is important to allow them space to communicate so that they feel heard. It is vital to stand back and listen intently from a neutral position without bringing your past experiences to the forefront–which can downgrade or discolour the conversation. Practise stepping into the other person's shoes for a moment while also being a compassionate witness. Feeling love and compassion for the other person, no matter how unfortunate their behaviour might be, can work wonders in turning things around.

I would like to share an experience where communication as a two-way street resolved a huge conflict. My friend looked like he was certainly going to have to go to court because his wife had broken all the rules for a collaborative divorce but a final meeting was proposed to see whether such a divorce could be salvaged. Every day leading up to the meeting, my friend only thought positive thoughts and envisioned a fair and equitable, ease and grace divorce for both parties. During the meeting, he listened intently to his wife's viewpoint, and her previous confrontational, aggressive and unforgiving approach was replaced with cooperation, understanding and peace. My friend's loving thoughts, leading up to and during the meeting, were being reflected back at him. His wife felt heard and supported him. At the end of the meeting that day, the two of them shared a taxi and even organised to meet and share a bottle of wine over dinner at some point.

Tools and techniques

For empowered communication, I have implemented the following tools and techniques with great success:

1. Personal, positive phrase first technique

I found it easier and more effective to communicate my needs by first introducing a positive phrase like, 'I like it when …' or 'it is important to me that …' Then I use a negative phrase about the behaviour I don't like, such as 'I don't like it when …' or 'I feel … when …'

I soon realised that speaking from my heart about how I genuinely felt caused the person to listen and had allowed me to be heard. I find this approach so much more effective than my past behaviour of letting loose with accusations and pointing the finger when things weren't as I liked.

2. Sandwich technique

This approach involves sandwiching your need between two positive statements.

Start with 'I love it when you …' Then state what you want, for example, 'what I would really like right now is …'

And add things like, 'thank you for doing …' or 'it makes such a difference to my day when you …'

3. Listen and reflect technique

An essential component for empowered communication is listening carefully to what is said and then immediately reflecting it back. Using the other person's words as much as possible makes this technique very powerful because the person feels that they have been heard and understood and not simply dismissed. After all, everyone loves to be seen, heard and understood.

Reflecting their words also gives you more opportunity to understand their viewpoint, how they feel and what they need. You can more easily step into their shoes. It also gives you time to digest what has been said so you can respond rather than react, which in turn helps pave the way for communication that is more respectful and cooperative–a win for both parties.

4. Timing is everything

I am sure most of us have been in situations where people have pounded us with requests at the most inconvenient times. The person receiving such communication is less likely to be agreeable. Bombarding your loved one with requests as soon as they walk in the door after a stressful day at the office, for example, is not likely to work in your favour. I often find that after dinner and a chance to unwind is the best time to communicate.

5. Hold the vision for the best possible result

It is paramount to visualise a positive outcome taking place. I think of how famous athletes, such as Roger Bannister, visualised winning and breaking a record–and then went on to do exactly that. If you feel you are going to be treated badly by your boss or partner, you probably will be because you will send out energy showing that's what you believe is going to happen. Your thoughts become your reality. Try visualising a positive outcome prior to your next meeting or discussion with your partner, co-worker or boss. You may surprise yourself at how powerful maintaining a positive outlook can be.

I started off experimenting with these techniques with my children regarding small annoying behaviours, such as garbage not being taken out and rooms not being cleaned. It wasn't long before I was ready to step up and effectively communicate on more confrontational issues, like when I felt a friend or loved one was disrespecting or taking advantage of me.

Over time and with practice, I found that communication of my needs became more empowered. Empowered communication didn't happen overnight but I tried not to beat myself up when I failed. I was practising and heading in the right direction. I recommend that you give these easy-to-implement approaches a chance.

To Sum Things Up

- empowered communication is an acquired skill, which takes courage, practice and determination to perfect;
- communication must be responsive, authentic, assertive, heartfelt and two-way to be effective; and
- applying five practical techniques helps ensure that communication is empowered.

CHAPTER 6

Me Time

Creation

In the stillness of night
Fiery passion whirls through my body,
Popping cells to life
Like baby firecrackers.

Passion pours out of me through a pen onto paper.
Words, colours. Shapes abound,
Surfacing to be acknowledged.
Hello Life Force.
I love you.
I move aside and allow
Creation to take place.

This is probably the most important chapter of the book. I feel that in our busy world, it is vital that we allow ourselves to slow down and take some much-needed daily time for ourselves, what I call, Me Time. This time is essential if we are to feel good. I try to recharge my batteries daily by doing something nourishing and that brings me joy–then I can align my flow and positive energy for the day. I see Me Time as having two equally essential components:

1. Quiet, reflective and meditative time.
2. Time to follow my joy.

Often for me, these two components are intertwined. For example, my painting or writing time is Me Time. It is meditative and brings me much joy. It is during Me Time that I gain a lot of clarity. I start to view problems from a more neutral perspective. It is a time when solutions start to emerge, often resolving the issues at hand. Allowing regular Me Time has also helped me develop a healthier sense of worth or self-esteem as I start to self-express and create. It has given me a sense of freedom to explore and get to know my true self.

Quiet, reflective time has several purposes. One of which is to allow negative emotions to surface so we can accept and move on from them. Not long after my separation, I went alone on a holiday to Airlie Beach in Queensland. Just being alone and not so caught up with life allowed me to be aware of my feelings as they welled up inside me. First, there was shock and anger, wondering why my husband thought he could divorce me after I had been so good to him for so many years. Then there was guilt and regret. I thought, maybe if I hadn't over-accommodated him and had spoken earlier of my needs, we would have had a more balanced relationship. Then there was sadness. I shed many tears for us not being able to grow old together. However, as each of these emotions came to the surface and was expressed, I felt a tremendous release and calmness. I definitely felt more at peace with the world.

The healing process took me three years, because it was easy to slip back into a victim mentality, pointing my finger at my ex-husband rather than working on making positive changes to and for myself. There were also the setbacks, as discussed in Chapter 2, where I chose to engage in activities that distracted me from how I really felt, instead of choosing to do something nurturing and proactive to help me on my healing journey. As I gradually started to heal, I began to have more clarity, seeing our relationship from a more neutral perspective. I saw that we really had grown apart and that we had differing needs.

Me Time also allows space for new experiences and opportunities. Alone time can feel awkward at first, especially if, like me, you have been a busy bee, rarely allowing yourself to stop. I experienced deep sadness and loneliness after spending nearly thirty years with my husband. In many ways, his going was like a death. I had no one in the evenings to share the happenings of the day with and no one to share my bed at night. There was also the inevitable fallout with those of our mutual friends who chose to take sides. It took a lot of practice and perseverance to feel comfortable with being alone and to allow space and time for my sadness to be expressed.

Gradually though, I began to cherish my alone time and to realise how important it was in the healing process. This quiet, reflective time was essential because it allowed space for new experiences and opportunities to emerge. Most of this book, including my poems and paintings, were created during this time alone. I was away from people and distractions, and immersed myself in nature, where I could reflect on what mattered most.

Stilling the busy mind

Most of us spend our whole lives with busy minds. This is emotionally exhausting. As I mentioned, we have up to 60,000 thoughts per day. Most thoughts tend to be about the past, which we can often do nothing about, or the future, which may never happen. Our minds can often go into negative, self-defeating mode. We think, *if only I was thinner, richer, more beautiful, healthier, wiser, freer, etc., I would be happy.* These thoughts waste vital energy that could be put to much better use, like healing the body and mind.

The exciting truth is, when we are in 'the now' through practising mindfulness or meditation, we are free of these thoughts. We get a break from the tireless tirade of energy-zapping contemplation. Most importantly, we begin to realise that it is only our monkey mind or our internal negative self-chatter that restrains us from living the life we want to live. These thoughts alone often stop us from exercising our own free will to dive deep into what we love and to put ourselves first.

I could have jumped on a plane and taken a holiday purely for me at many times over the years. So, what had stopped me? Me! My monkey mind had imprisoned me and stopped me from being free to be me. I needed to be free to hear myself, be aware of my emotions, my true needs and, most importantly, to meet my needs by communicating them effectively.

Freedom

Inhale.
Sip the sweetness of life into every cell.
Hold. Be still.
Invigorate, expand.
Release slowly,
Gifting the shackles of life into Mother Earth.
Give thanks.
You are free.

Meditation

Why meditate? Most of us can readily come up with a range of excuses: it's boring; there's no time; it's a waste of time; it puts me to sleep; I don't know how; it doesn't do anything for me; I'd rather be making money, exercising or enjoying myself partying with my friends; it's only for hippies. The list goes on and on. I'll let you in on a secret that you may not know: meditation is the way back to the real you and an amazing life. It's your power to free yourself from behaviours, beliefs and habits that no longer serve you.

Daily meditation frees you from the conditioned subconscious mind and gives you more clarity, not tainted by past events, behaviours or beliefs. You are more productive and time-efficient with tasks, and your intuition and ability to see the bigger picture and others' perspectives also become more developed. I have been meditating for only three years, so am still excited and intrigued by what the future holds.

Meditation is the gateway to your soul and unleashes your creativity. Creative arts that you never imagined you could possibly enjoy, let alone be accomplished at, can come to the forefront if you are open to trying them. Strength, flexibility and mobility are also greatly improved as the body is 'freed up.' Meditation lifts your spirits or, more specifically, uplifts you to a higher vibration or consciousness. It allows you to feel and experience your true essence, peace, love and even bliss. People in a lower consciousness tend to leave your life, while those on a higher consciousness enter it. You get into the flow with opportunities that improve your wellbeing as well as the wellbeing of others. Those around you, including your loved ones, receive the benefits of you feeling good with a higher vibration.

Participating in Kundalini, the self-awareness yoga, or other forms of yoga or exercise also expedite the benefits of meditation. I was introduced to Kundalini by my good friend, Valerie. (Yes, the same girlfriend who taught me the Boundary Self-Check Test.) This practice assists in freeing up energy within us which spirals up from the base of the spine. (Please refer to Appendices 3 and 4 for more discussion on this form of yoga.) A book I recommend on this practice is *Ancient Teachings for Beginners* by Douglas De Long.

Today, my life is abundant in so many ways, which I believe is due to meditation. I enjoy perfect health, amazing clarity of thought and great intuition. I have come across painting and writing but am open to exploring other creative arts in the future. I have always been flexible but my flexibility has dramatically improved.

Meditation allows you to be in the now, appreciating sensations, sounds, sights, smells, thoughts and feelings as they are taking place. It allows your problems to take a back seat as you still the monkey mind.

Meditation can take many forms. For some of us, it's sitting upright in a crossed-leg position; for others, it's a walk in the park, a rest on the couch or under a tree, a swim in the sea or staring at the stars. It doesn't matter what form meditation takes. Any still, alone time, ideally in contact with nature, that enables us to listen, to be in the now and to feel how we feel, will in turn tell us what we need to be free and happy–which is everyone's birthright.

Tools for meditation

Deep breathing

Many of us, particularly at first, find it difficult to meditate. In the early days, my yoga teacher was constantly telling me to think of nothing but that would lead to even more thoughts whirling around in my head. Rather than let my mind drift to my to-do lists and recurrent problems, I would instead focus on my breathing, which is instinctive and helpful.

In the rushed, stressed-out world in which many of us live, we tend to shallow breathe from the chest area rather than the belly. Effective breathing activates our parasympathetic nervous system. This is powerful healing for the body as it stops excessive cortisol production. Our body registers that we are safe and moves away from the fight or flight response to one of rest, digestion, repair, reproduction and creation. Some important benefits of deep breathing are listed below, though this is by no means an exhaustive list. I highly recommend Anders Olsson's book, *Conscious Breathing*, for more detailed discussion on the optimal breathing technique and benefits.

- Reduced stress and anxiety as mind and body are more relaxed.
- Release of endorphins or feel-good hormones, which act as a natural painkiller.
- Less acidity in the body, hence less potential for disease.
- Improved sleeping.
- Increased lung capacity.
- Improved nervous and immune system function.
- Optimal blood pressure.
- Increased life expectancy.

The tool of simply breathing improves our overall state of health and wellbeing in so many ways. We do need some cortisol as it helps us get up in the morning, get the most from a workout and is vital for the health of our nervous system. However, too much can be damaging and, if continually over-produced, it keeps us in a stressed-out state, which can lead to exhaustion, burnout and depression. So, how do we effectively breathe?

1. Stand or sit with your spine as comfortably straight as possible, chin tucked in slightly and looking ahead.
2. If practical, close your eyes and breathe in, gently sucking in as much air into your lungs as you comfortably can.
3. Your shoulders may try to rise but resist that. Instead, think of expanding your lungs sideways and broadening your back while keeping your shoulders down.
4. Your stomach should expand and deflate with every breath, as your diaphragm moves down and up.

5. Breathe in deeply and slowly through your nose for four seconds, hold for three, then breathe out through your nose for eight seconds and hold for a further three. The number of seconds you breathe in and out can be increased over time but it is important to exhale for about twice as long as you inhale each time.
6. As you breathe in, think of bringing fresh, revitalising oxygen and energy into every cell of your being. As you breathe out, think of letting go of the day, your worries and concerns. Try visualising all your stress being sent down to Mother Earth through the soles of your feet and base of your spine.
7. Breathe for five minutes, or longer if possible, using this technique.
8. Note how you feel. (Right afterwards is a great time to journal anything that comes up, such as ideas, thoughts or emotions.)
9. Repeat the above steps as much as possible during the day–at stop lights, in queues, before important meetings; until it becomes a habit.

Practise consistently with this breathing technique for six weeks, and it will replace your old breathing pattern for good and become automatic. Watch how your wellbeing improves as your nervous system gets a reboot.

Mantra

The science of mantra chanting is being recognised as an extremely powerful tool for meditation, as discussed in Dr Kulreet Chaudhary's *Sound Medicine: How to Use the Ancient Science of Sound to Heal the Body and Mind.* Should you wish to explore mantra more fully, I highly recommend her book. Especially effective are Sanskrit mantras that use individual *bija* or seed sounds that correspond to specific energies. According to Dr Chaudhary, 'seed mantras were created to encompass sounds that cannot be translated into literal meaning but utilise the power of tonal vibration to create balance and peace in the body and mind.'

I find that these sounds assist me in diving deep into my true self while being less distracted by the noise of my thoughts.

For mantras to be effective, it is important that you are in the right zone. Make sure you are comfortable, seated upright and that you aren't wearing any restrictive clothing around your belly. Take three long, deep breaths, breathing in fully. When you slowly release each time, make the vocal sound *Om*.

According to Dr Chaudhary, '[the *Om*] mantra is the most basic of all mantras, yet it's the most important one: It is the source of all other mantras and is believed to contain all vibratory sounds. This all-encompassing sound of creation is found in the beginning of nearly all mantras. The word, or primordial sound, *Om/Aum* in the Vedas (the oldest religious texts originating in ancient India) which is correlative to Amen in Christianity, Hum in Tibetan and Amin in Islam, is also sometimes referred to as the word of God.'

Think of letting go of all your current stresses and worries. Next, imagine breathing the vibration or sound of the mantra into the centre of your chest, thinking of someone you really love. It could be a partner or child, your pet or Mother Nature. This is a vital step as it activates and opens your heart chakra, allowing you to tap more readily into your true essence or soul. Imagine holding your loved one in your heart chakra during your chant. You are not limited to chanting three *Om*s. (See Appendices 4 and 5, Further Reading and Resources, for information on chanting, mantras and group practice.)

The benefits of deep breathing discussed above are enhanced by adopting this or any recognised mantra. Dr Chaudhary expands on the benefits of chanting, including 'relaxing and rejuvenating the mind, thereby increasing concentration and memory and your ability to learn; and eliminating negative repetitive thoughts as well as helping to decrease stress and promote social connections.'

When starting with mantras, it is best to chant externally. As you become more comfortable, you can start to chant internally. Breathing techniques can also be incorporated into internal mantra chanting. Don't worry if your mind drifts away from the mantra; simply allow yourself to come back to it without judgement. There was a worldwide mantra offered by my Guru for the 2019 Australian bushfires and there is one for the COVID-19 pandemic, which is currently being chanted in major cities around the world. Called the 'Maha Kali Mantra' by Amma, it is a powerful mantra for destroying negativity and disease within you as well as the broader community. It can currently be accessed via soundcloud.com.

Chanting as a group is more powerful, as positive vibrations are amplified, benefiting not only those chanting but also the world. Dr Chaudhary's book discusses a broad range of healing mantras that you can select from, depending on what particular ailment or challenge you are experiencing.

In addition to chanting and effective breathing, here are some tools to remain in the present moment:

- be aware of your five senses;
- recognise that every time your thoughts go into negative mode, you are often thinking about the past or the future, and that these thoughts involve events and experiences that have already happened or may not happen;
- be grateful for the things that bring joy to your life right now; and
- focus on what you have, rather than what you don't have.

Journaling is also a great way to focus on your thoughts and feelings to gain some clarity and to work at resolving problems and conflict. Writing about how you feel alerts you to your needs and sends you in the right direction to meet them. A gratitude diary is also a great tool, because being grateful and thankful for things tends to lead to more great things being attracted into your life. Writing about and visualising your utopic life as though it is happening is also a very powerful tool and I discuss this further in the next chapter.

True Essence is my first abstract painting and was created at a time when I was experiencing uplifting emotions of love and peace and feeling wonderfully supported. Cyndi, my beautiful art teacher, laid out her rules clearly. There were none. We could have a shape or colour concept to run with but that was about it. We were encouraged to let loose on our canvas. I didn't really know what I was creating and just went with the moment. I feel this is a wonderful analogy for how we should view life. It's much easier, and I believe more beneficial, to go with the flow of what you are experiencing now, rather than attaching to a structured, fixed idea of what you want or expect in the future. Such attachments can lead to undue distress and can impede the flow of better opportunities.

It's worth saying that I first met my husband because I had acted on my intuition, passing up an organised end-of-financial-year work dinner to spontaneously attend a black-tie function with a girlfriend instead. I just felt that was where I should be at that time. The phone had rung literally as I was leaving for the work dinner, and I had run back inside and changed to go with my girlfriend. Intuition guided me. And, despite the divorce, I recognise that I have four beautiful children and much more of life's wisdom as a result of our twenty-five-year marriage together.

True Essence

Time to follow your joy

We all truly need to implement our own system for self-love. This means dedicating time to follow exactly what nourishes you and makes your heart sing. Until we can care for, fully accept and love ourselves, we are not in a position to care for and truly love another. To be capable of receiving and giving love unconditionally, we must start with loving ourselves first.

Oprah Winfrey, in her book *What I Know for Sure*, writes, 'my biggest mistakes in life have all stemmed from giving my power away to someone else … believing that the love others had to offer was more important than the love I had to give myself.' I wish I had received this wisdom as a child, to put my love for myself first. What if parents were to ask their young child who she loved most in the world, and when she responded, 'Mummy and Daddy,' the parents gently remind her, 'no, you love yourself more than anything in the world.' This would have a positive impact on the wellbeing and mental health of that child.

Over the past three years, I have adopted a variety of transformational tools and self-love practices (which are listed in Appendices 2 and 3) and I find them extremely effective in restoring a healthy, loving sense of self that recharges me, so that I am in a position to give and share with others, uplifting them.

As I dive deep into what I love, I discover more about myself. The old me would never have stopped in her busy day to feel and express her emotions. Neither would she have allowed herself to do something that genuinely made her happy, particularly if she thought she was neglecting her duties as mother and wife.

Choosing to follow my joy has been my power. In discovering hidden talents and engaging more fully in passions and hobbies, I am slowly building my self-worth. As a result, I am now beginning to recognise and meet my needs. I am finally putting myself first and stepping up and into my ultimate life. It takes courage to dive into something new, like taking up painting or writing this book, and I have found that you really need to ignore your inner dialogue of 'I can't. I shouldn't. I am going to embarrass myself' and follow your heart. My reward has been discovering myself, as well as having lots of fun while doing it.

Child's play

I believe that true self-expression does not care about the audience and what other people are thinking. Young children don't paint or model clay to please others but rather to please themselves. An effective way to discover what makes you happy is to tap into your inner child and remember what you enjoyed when you were young. I love Julia Cameron's book and course, *The Artist's Way*, which deals with ways of awakening the child within you. Many of us have lost sight of what truly makes our heart sing but by playing with creative hobbies that we enjoyed growing up, like dancing, writing, music, a particular sport, cooking, drawing or painting, we can awaken our true creative selves.

I remember my eight-year-old self making a pact with my closest girlfriend at the time (who years later became my bridesmaid). We said, 'if we can still play on the swings and the monkey bars, we will always have fun and never grow old.' My childhood self was right. She was saying, 'don't be afraid to have fun. Always express your authentic self and never lose track of who you truly are.' But my adult self took a long time to understand this truth.

Following a healthy eating plan

The moment I returned from a month in India in May 2019, I knew I wanted to paint–one of the central practices of my Me Time. However, I was also intent on improving my diet and eating behaviours. The trip had been my longest to date because I'd been determined to cleanse my body and mind. I'd stayed at a recently established Holistic Centre established by my Guru, Amma. The vision of the centre is 'to transform the individual through an inward healing process of the body, mind and spirit that in turn inspires transformation in the world through greater understanding of the interconnectedness between the health of the individual, the health of the environment and the health of our communities.' (Please refer to Appendix 5 for more information on the centre.)

This retreat offered daily yoga practice, Ayurvedic and Siddha medicines, with meditation, various therapy and information sessions and a purely vegetarian diet. Whether our food is to fully energise and nourish us depends not only on what we eat but also how we prepare it, and when and how we consume it. Many of us realise that fresh, organic and unprocessed food is best. My stay at the Holistic Centre also brought other realisations. I now understand how overcooking and the use of microwaves destroy valuable nutrients, and also that the way in which food is consumed is important–sitting down to eat with a grateful and calm demeanour, eating slowly, not being distracted by screens or people, all enable our bodies to effectively accept and absorb the nutrients. The Ayurvedic approach to eating and diet is to consume the largest meal in the morning and the lightest at an early dinner before sunset, so that energy can be directed to healing the body during the night rather than used for digesting food.

I truly believe food can be great medicine for our bodies. I recently completed a nine-day liver cleanse as detailed in Anthony William's book, *Medical Medium Liver Rescue*. After the nine days, my LDL (bad) cholesterol had dramatically reduced to acceptable levels, and I felt more energised and lighter, both physically and mentally.

I highly recommend Anthony William and Dr Vasant Lad's book, *Ayurveda: The Science of Self-Healing*, should you wish to explore the Ayurvedic approach to better health. I also suggest Gillian McKeith's books, *Food Bible: How to Use Food to Cure What Ails You* and *You Are What You Eat: The Plan That Will Change Your Life*. (All books are referenced in Appendix 4.)

After my time in India, I had better health and energy levels, as well as more clarity and focus on my life's direction. I clearly knew that I wanted to include my paintings in this book. Certainly prior to my first trip to India, I would have thought taking up painting a preposterous idea. Society does not usually encourage us to feel our emotions, or to express and act upon how we feel–but if we can tap into our emotions and follow what we love, our hearts open and we connect more with our soul's power. From this vantage point of a healthy body and clearer mind, life is blissful, peaceful, free, satisfying and joyous.

Benefits of Me Time

Me Time is paramount to finding the real you. It helps you to gain a sense of self, what you like, what you don't like and what makes you happy. It allows you to identify your needs, wants and desires. It also helps you feel good, which raises your vibration. As you continue to follow your joy, diving into what makes you happy, you start to identify creative talents often previously hidden from you and the world.

We all have creative talents waiting to be tapped. As you discover more about the real you, as you deepen into a practice of Me Time you will start to build your self-worth. This, in turn, will enable you to step into your power, enforce boundaries and communicate your needs effectively. It is at this time that issues and problems will start dissolving, or at least being viewed from a neutral perspective so as not to overwhelm you. It is then that the ultimate life will open its gates to you.

For many of us, our emotional body or inner child has been forgotten or neglected. However, when we revive this part of ourselves, we are alerted to our needs and how to experience a sense of wellbeing. That inner child is also the well that holds our creativity.

Unfortunately, most of us don't stop in our busy day to feel our emotions and do something that genuinely makes us happy. You have to be brave and allow yourself to be vulnerable, sitting with your negative thoughts and emotions. It is tempting to stay on the easy, familiar road, numbing yourself and ignoring your true needs. However, this can lead to your inner child having tantrums or meltdowns–but if we practise Me Time, we can soothe the inner child. We can free ourselves and live the life we have always wanted.

To Sum Things Up

Me Time has two equally essential components: time to be quiet and reflect and time to follow your joy.

Me Time allows me to:

- identify my needs and discover creative talents;
- heal and view life from a neutral standpoint;
- experience a true sense of joy and overall wellbeing;
- develop my sense of worth;
- step into my power;
- free myself from restrictive patterns and behaviours; and
- rediscover or remember the true me

Note-taking page for self-reflection

CHAPTER 7

Letting Go and Forgiveness

Face of Change

Let go.
Be curious,
Courageous.
Step towards
Not away from
Darkness into Light.
Embrace,
Uplift others.
In Flow
Love Peace Bliss.

Let Go

Charles Darwin said, 'it is not the strongest species that survive, nor the most intelligent, but the ones most responsive to change.'

This quote resonates with me. I believe that to change and to be free to fly, you must give up on everything that weighs you down. I think of the pelican, especially the one who has recently been visiting me at my home. This beautiful bird symbolises the need to let go of habits that don't serve us, along with behaviours, patterns and limiting beliefs, to make space for new and better things. The pelican has a large pouch which it uses to fish. It knows when to empty this pouch so that it can take to the skies effortlessly.

Letting go of my past over-accommodating behaviour is paramount. I also need to let go of my attachment to the family home that we had for many years. Now, with half of my children moved into their own homes, I hope to let our family home go and find my own home that's right for me. I imagine it will be liberating, similar to when, as the children reached driving age, I finally replaced the family bus with a car of my own that met my requirements. My marriage and the family home served me well, allowing me to bring up four amazing children but it's time to love and let go, and it's time to grow.

Once we have mastered listening to our emotions and recognising our needs, we start to become aware of things that are standing in our path, stopping us from stepping forward to claim our best life for ourselves. Unless we can let go of things that are not serving us, there will be little opportunity to let in the good stuff. I like the analogy of walking up a cold, draughty corridor and that unless we can fully shut the door behind us on what is not working, the draught from that door will jam shut the door of opportunity ahead of us. Consider letting go of:

1. Toxic relationships.
2. Restrictive behavioural patterns or habits.
3. Negative self-talk.
4. Unforgiveness.

Toxic relationships at home and in the workplace

Most of us have endured a toxic relationship at some time in our life, whether it's with a boss, co-worker, partner, parent or child. They are relationships that tend to suffocate, rather than support you; they restrict, rather than allow you to grow and be free to be you. They are relationships where love is conditional.

Once you have recognised these relationships as toxic, it's up to you to deal with them. A good start is to establish boundaries as to which behaviours are acceptable and which are not. It is vital to enforce these boundaries and follow through with consequences if they are broken. One consequence may mean letting go of that relationship. (Please refer to Chapters 4 and 5 on Boundaries and Communication.)

Most of us spend at least half of our waking life either in education or work of some form, so I feel it is important that both serve you as much as your education and work serve others. It is important that you are putting yourself first. Do you look forward to work each morning? If not, what can you do about it? If you are not enjoying work, it is probably sapping your energy and you are unlikely to be working at optimal capacity. If that's the case, you have a few choices:

1. Change nothing. Continue in your current employment, steadily exhausting your energy reserve until you're reduced to a shell.
2. Speak up and implement some changes that make your work more tolerable and enjoyable for you, such as setting clear boundaries.
3. Look for another job that makes your heart sing.

It takes tremendous courage to leave your job. After all, you may not get another one, and that is likely to have financial implications. Even though your heart may know that your current job is not the one for you, your ego is likely to be persistent in talking you out of making a change. I found this to be my experience when I had just qualified as a chartered accountant but decided to delve into primary school teaching. My work colleagues thought I had gone mad, giving up my new, lucrative career. However, I knew that I had to take action because I wasn't thriving–I was working for a big accounting organisation in audit and insolvency, and barely surviving. My ego tried hard to sway me to stay with its tireless tirade of internal negative chatter: *you are too old to go back to university. You won't survive without your pay packet. Teachers are overworked and underpaid. What are you thinking?*

Of course, the change you make does not have to be as dramatic as mine was. In the end, my Diploma of Education prepared me for raising my own children and to pursue mentoring later on. Most importantly, though, it brought me closer to finding what made my heart sing and what did not. I was starting to speak up for what I wanted.

What's important is that your heart is at the helm–not your head–when making important lifestyle choices and decisions. Your head is a good copilot but your heart should be the driver if you aspire to a vocation that fills you with joy. The bonus is that a job that makes your heart sing will most likely result in better health. It may even lead to more wealth, as you are more likely to be talented in this area, as well as focused and driven, and you will likely work at full capacity and optimum productivity. Changes to employment don't need to be made overnight. Maybe your change will involve igniting a favourite hobby at the weekend, which can gently slip into your working week over time. Be courageous and open to opportunities, and your heart will guide you.

Restrictive behavioural patterns and habits

To really free yourself, you have to move away from the expectations of your parents, your peers, your teachers and loved ones. As I've shared before, I am the older child and have always wanted nothing more than the love and adoration of my parents. To some degree, subconsciously, I was always looking for their approval of what to do and when. Like many of us, I was conditioned to be of use, doing things that were met with others' approval or following what was safe. This behaviour, I have come to realise, was a subconscious program running in my head.

After separating from my husband, I was determined to delve further into understanding how I could lose myself. From four years of age, I had always kept everyone happy, fully accommodating my parents, my younger sister, my teachers and later my sexual partners. I excelled in most subjects and sports at school and went on to university. Not truly knowing what I wanted to study, I took business as a safe option encouraged by my father. He would say, 'commerce is a great base if you are unsure what you want to do; it is always something you can fall back into if you need it.' I had agreed with him at the time, thinking it was a great idea.

However, once I qualified as a chartered accountant, I found that it didn't bring me joy. That career was simply not me. It was potentially lucrative but the thought of pursuing it made me sick to my stomach. With the support of my husband, I summoned the courage to go back to university and pursue primary school teaching. My peers–and to a certain degree, my parents–might have thought that I had turned mad but the prospect filled me with joy, and I dived into it, following my heart. My teaching career was short-lived because I started my family within three years of marriage and created my own little primary school by having four children within five years. I then continued on the journey of losing myself by putting my husband's and children's needs before mine for the next twenty years.

I can now reflect with clarity that I had simply forgotten about myself as I cared for my parents, teachers, husband and children. I had yearned for and received their approval and love but nowhere had I stopped to explore what I really loved or taken the time to follow my dreams. I now realise I had rarely met my own needs due to feelings of unworthiness. I had simply lost myself under the masks of daughter, student, chartered accountant, wife, mother, personal assistant and cook. Also, I had inevitably become invisible not only to myself but to my husband as well.

I believe that it is often our intrinsic restrictive patterns or behaviours that cause some part of our life to become toxic. These patterns and behaviours can be difficult to identify at first, especially if they have been with us since we were very young. We can usually see these restrictive patterns and behaviours in others but not in ourselves.

It is very easy to point the finger at someone else, saying it's their problem and that they need to change, rather than looking at yourself and changing by letting go of your restrictive patterns and behaviours. I believe that if we don't recognise our restrictive behaviour and we fail to speak up when things are not as we like, we have only ourselves to blame. (Please revisit Chapter 5 for tools for empowered communication, if you are struggling with this issue.)

Negative self-talk

Negative self-talk prevents us from living our highest joy. I believe that in the subconscious of many people, there is the belief that they are not worthy. This belief manifests itself in negative thoughts, such as the fear of letting people down, the fear of how other people will perceive us and the fear of not being good enough. We spend a great deal of mental energy focusing on how we perceive people are going to perceive us!

As a teenager, I often had thoughts that I didn't fit in, that no one would want to hang out with me or would be interested in what I had to say. These thoughts not only drained me but they created my reality causing my peers to keep their distance, likely reflecting my low vibes of unworthiness. My thoughts at the time were definitely preventing me from experiencing joy.

The Buddha said, 'the mind is everything. What you think, you become.'

Often, negative self-talk is an internal dialogue that has been going on for a long time. It takes a discerning awareness to recognise it, and then to be able to let it go. Letting go requires practice and commitment. The best way to quiet this monkey mind of negative self-talk is through some form of meditation or quiet time. Remember, meditation allows you to see with clarity that these unloving thoughts are just thoughts; they are not the real you. (Please revisit to Chapter 6 for Me Time, for further discussion on meditation.)

Non-forgiveness

Nothing burdens you more than not forgiving others. Choosing not to forgive someone burdens the heart, causing much distress. Non-forgiveness causes dis-ease and can, I believe, lead to disease if not addressed. I am not saying that we should condone misbehaviour or violence but I have learnt that allowing myself to forgive and have compassion for the perpetrator allows my heart to heal and my health to flourish.

Initially, I found it too difficult to forgive my ex-husband because I was experiencing too much sadness and anger. My counsellor encouraged me to 'fake it until you make it' with forgiveness. Over time, I was able to truly forgive my husband and myself, and I think he forgave me as well. This allowed us both to move forward without heaviness in our hearts.

Dr Viktor Frankl, a survivor of the horrors of Auschwitz and author of *Man's Search for Meaning*, writes of how he used to practise sending love and peace to his captors. He refused to feel hatred and vengeance, because he knew it was foreign to his true self and would only burden him and impact his health detrimentally.

Recently, I had my wallet stolen. I could have gone into a drama, asking, 'why me?' But what good would that have done, except to make me feel worse or feel more like a victim? So, I turned it around. I prayed that the person who 'received' my wallet could now feed themself and their family. I even did a forgiveness mantra, forgiving the thief and forgiving myself. I immediately felt a lot better as I had let the anger, frustration and fear go.

This practice of forgiveness requires courage and sometimes a leap of faith, as well as a willingness to let go of patterns and routines that don't serve you. Although these patterns may have kept us safe in the past, they won't help us in the long term.

I thought my girlfriend was overreacting when my husband filed for divorce but she urged me to see a lawyer and offered to come along. I was sure that my husband was going to realise what a mistake he was making and would change his mind. *It's just a matter of time*, I told myself. I didn't want to face the fact that he wanted a divorce. He had not even given me a reason why and I think my initial dismissal and disbelief kept me from plummeting into deep fear, despair, heartache and depression.

No one I knew from my generation had divorced, which probably heightened my worries but over time, I started to come to the realisation that I was indeed getting divorced. When I summoned the courage to go to the lawyer's office with my friend, I soon realised that the Universe had my back. By engaging my lawyer, I was taking steps to free myself from a relationship that no longer met my needs. I then began to feel safe and quietly confident that I was finally taking the reins and heading in the right direction.

I believe that any heartfelt moves that you have the courage to make, particularly if they also bring joy to others, will be supported by the Universe. I have seen time and time again how people, myself included, flourish once they can detach and find the courage to walk away from unsatisfactory work or home situations. It is then that there is space for new opportunities, such as their true vocation or a better partner, to come to fruition.

Tools to help let go

Forgiveness is a vital ingredient in letting go of the past, which allows space for more positive experiences because healing and growth can take place. Forgiving and having compassion also help to heal those you love or who challenge your love. I find this three-way forgiveness mantra a most effective tool in freeing all concerned. It was taught to me by Anjani Amriit, my first spiritual teacher. (Please refer to Appendix 4 for her website.) The mantra involves:

1. Asking for forgiveness.
2. Forgiving the other person or people.
3. Forgiving yourself for pain and suffering caused.

There are many forgiveness mantras that can be found online, so you can easily choose one that inspires you. I definitely feel a lot lighter after I say this mantra. It allows me to move on, release past traumas and live in the now, rather than continuing to hold onto the past, which would constrain my growth. I have found that forgiveness also assists the other party in helping them to cut loose from the past and free themselves. If possible, the act of forgiving can be done in person, making the process even more effective.

Immediately after my divorce, forgiveness seemed absolutely impossible. I was too angry that my idealised future of adventuring and growing old together with our grandchildren around us had been stripped from me. But over time, I began to recognise that it was me and my behaviour that had attracted the negative things into my life in the first place. This revelation helped me to be more enthusiastic and genuine with my forgiveness mantra going forward.

Ho'oponopono, the ancient Hawaiian practice of forgiveness, is another powerful tool. This powerful healing and forgiveness mantra was developed by Dr Ihaleakala Hew Len. By constantly repeating this mantra, he healed four of his clients–hospitalised in a mental institution–by healing himself. The words are:

I am sorry,
Please forgive me,
Thank you,
I love you.

Variations can be found online, accompanied by a range of different tunes. The lyrics remain the same, although the order of the phrases can vary.

How do I let go?

Me Time not only provides clarity on resolving challenges and problems but it also instils courage and offers guidance when it comes to change and letting go. Listening to my inner child, with some discipline from my adult self, is incredibly useful. Specifically, activities like meditation, yoga, painting or simply taking time out from the busy world help me let go of what's not working and to focus on what *is*. Chanting a forgiveness mantra also helps me let go of any grudges or resentments as they surface.

During Me Time, feelings of grief, anger, fear, guilt, shame, regret or resentment come to the surface. Sometimes these feelings manifest as sensations, aches or pains in my body, like a sore back or shoulder, a tight hip or an aching knee. As difficult as it may seem, I try to sit with the sensation or emotion that arises. I allow myself to be curious, lovingly asking what the emotion or sensation is trying to tell me. What does it need or what does it want me to learn? These sensations and emotions are assisting me in moving into a better mind space. I think of them as my guardian angels, and I try my best to be thankful for them.

As discussed in Chapter 4, these negative feelings signal that something isn't right and that I need to change things or let go to be happy and free; that I need to step away from past restrictive behaviours and step up to a more empowered self. When my friends and family have accidents or become ill, it is often they are overworking or overindulging and not listening to what is best for them; they are often not acknowledging their emotions or speaking up and putting themselves first.

As my mother often tells me, 'when things start to overwhelm you, have a good cry and let it all out and you will feel better.' This advice sounds simplistic but often a good cry or time to reflect and sit with the pain allows it to surface and move on. Bringing repressed emotions to the surface allows us to heal.

Today, as I become aware of all my restrictive patterns and habits, I choose to let them go. I choose to see the goodness in everyone. I try not to rescue, control, or judge but instead to allow those I love to follow their own paths and grow. I tap into my intuition, listen to my heart and try to go with the flow of my ever-changing life. I aim to accept things that I cannot change. I view problems not as obstacles but as opportunities for growth. I step up and speak my truth on things that matter and that I can change. As a result, fresh opportunities that are empowering tend to readily flow into my life.

I love the Serenity Prayer, originally written by the American theologian and author, Reinhold Niebuhr, which now reads, 'God, grant me the serenity to accept the things I cannot change, the courage to change the things I can, and the wisdom to know the difference.'

To Sum Things Up

Letting go of:

- toxic relationships;
- restrictive behavioural patterns and habits;
- negative self-talk; and
- non-forgiveness

... allows me to make space for better more empowering relationships and behaviours.

Tools: Forgiveness Mantras and Me Time

Note-taking page for self-reflection

CHAPTER 8

Gratitude and Embracing Change

Wise One

Wise One

You greet me at my gate
On my twins' birthday night.
Your presence astounds me.
I am transfixed by your beauty.

Such knowledge and wisdom
You impart.

Change is upon me
And all.
So Be It.

On the evening of my twins' twentieth birthday in 2019, as I returned from dinner, I was greeted by an owl perched on my front gate. I was immediately drawn to this beautiful proud bird. For me, the owl symbolises that a life transition or change is imminent. Little did I know that we were to be hit soon with the worst bushfires in Australia's history, as well as a worldwide pandemic.

The owl also symbolises wisdom and intuition. We are always going to have challenges, both on an individual and worldwide level; however, I also believe that no matter how difficult life becomes at times, the Universe has our back. My teen years, the period of my chronic back pain, and my divorce were very challenging times but in retrospect, they were all opportunities to grow, to speak up, to stand up and to claim my life as my own.

Certainly, at the time of writing this, the current COVID-19 pandemic is one large challenge that humanity is facing. However, Mother Earth is getting a chance to revive herself, and we are all being given an opportunity to assess what's working and what's not in our lives and in the world at large. I believe there is a growing sense of community and connectivity as people work tirelessly to treat and care for one another and to find vaccines and a cure. I feel many of us are reassessing our priorities, examining what is meaningful and important in our lives and letting go of things that don't bring us joy.

I have found that when uncomfortable things arise that I cannot change–and there will always be many such things–I am better off accepting them. When I go with the current of life rather than resisting it, I experience less discomfort. Solutions and opportunities open up more readily. I try to focus on what's working and being thankful, which brings in more abundance.

Gratitude

Gratitude

Thank you for the birds that sing.
Thank you for everything.

Thank you for showering me with blessings and grace.
Thank you, Akasha, for holding me in place.

Please guide me how to best serve humanity.
I surrender to you my ego and insanity.

I pray to uplift to more peace and love,
Beloved Amma, I seek truth from above.

Like the ebb and flow of the sea
Is our love exchange, my Beloved and I am free.

Expressing gratitude daily

The more I focus on being thankful for the things I have, rather than things I don't have, the more things come my way to be thankful about. When I stop and express gratitude, I feel so much love and peace in my heart, and it radiates to others. Every morning, I thank the Universe for my life and for my family and friends and for the opportunity to uplift others by sharing my joy, whether that is through serving them or by being joyful around them.

I am grateful to my parents for bringing me into the world. They were my first teachers. They continue to nurture, love and protect me. They regularly instil in me the belief that I can achieve anything I set my mind to and that I should follow my dreams. Over the past five years, and after much self-reflection, I realise that I am thankful to my former husband. I was brought up to believe that marriage was for life; however, my divorce has liberated me by allowing me to find me.

I am grateful to have been blessed with four beautiful, loving children who are now adults, freely exploring and discovering themselves. They keep teaching me so much about life. They mirror any problems or obstacles that I am not tackling effectively. They nourish and enrich my life every day, for which I hold so much gratitude. I am grateful to live in a country where fresh food and clean water are readily available, allowing me to nourish my body and help it function at its best.

I am thankful to be able to explore foreign countries. I enjoyed living as a child in London, and later with my family in Tokyo and Vanuatu. I have spent time in Europe and Asia. More recently, I have made regular trips to India, where the beautiful country and its people give me a chance to hone in on the fabric of life. There, I can feel my emotional body and tap into my powerful self. I come away from India recharged, with a powerful drive to create and explore more, coupled with contentment and being grounded.

Although many Indian families struggle to feed, clothe and shelter themselves and there is much suffering, I am always drawn to the broad smiles of Indian children living so simply and freely. I see how many of us in the developed world lose ourselves in the fast pace of life, pursuing things that are often meaningless and joyless. Even though we may be blessed to have our basic needs met, we can become entrapped in our materialistic world, wanting more to feel content.

My time in India has also allowed me to understand that we are all souls having a human experience and that we each have our own character. When I am able to tap into my soul through my heart, whether that's through meditation, music, nature or any experience that fills me with joy and love, I feel at one with the world. It is in this joyous and peaceful state that I am most creative. This divine energy or feeling is what I love to share with my family, friends and acquaintances.

And this joyous, loving, peaceful state is within each of us. Our true essence and our loving awareness are always there; we must take the time and the opportunity to tap into it. I feel many of us need to remember that we are all created equal and live on Mother Earth under one sun. We need to fully embrace and respect the wisdom of the First Nations and the Indigenous people wherever we live, so we can move forward together as one united human race.

With our self-awareness, we can each grow in our own way, supporting the paradigm shift from a world of inequality, materialism, fear and intolerance to one of equality, connection, understanding and love. By healing ourselves, we can work together to create a better world. We need to look within to our own inner fears and demons, acknowledging, accepting and letting them go. We are then in a better position to dismantle the inequalities and misunderstandings of race, gender and religion that have prevailed for so long and that have caused, and continue to cause, so much human suffering. Each of us has an important part to play in this work.

I hope the tools within this book will assist you on your transformational journey, so you can be free to put yourself first and unlock your ultimate life–and thus uplift the lives of your loved ones and those around you.

Koolewong

One year after the devastation of the Australian bushfires of 2019, I was blessed to get up close and personal with a koala in the hinterland of Byron Bay. I have named the painting *Koolewong*, an Aboriginal word for koala, paying my respects to the original custodians of this beautiful land.

Our Australia

Our lives are short.
We run like frantic animals in fear,
Focusing on earning and controlling,
Not on loving.

Disconnected from Mother Nature
We grasp onto material possessions.
Do they make us happy?
For a short time maybe.

We enter and leave this world alone.
It is only the love in our hearts that endures.
We neglect the elements of life, essential for our existence:
The air we breathe, the earth we stand on,
The water we drink,
The fiery sun and ether that energise us.

When are we to finally unite as one
To bring healing to Our Australia?
Let's bring together
The knowledge of the New Australians
With the knowings of the First Nation's people.
What a wonderful Australia we could be.

To Sum Things Up

- it takes courage, but it is better to embrace change and other difficulties rather than to resist them;
- problems, when addressed rather than ignored, tend to diminish and help us to grow and claim our life as our own;
- gratitude for things in our life brings more good things; and
- we are all unique beings, and together we can make the world a better place.

CONCLUSION

Looking Ahead

Shine Brightly

Shine Brightly

The lighthouse beams its light and love afar,
Firmly grounded to Mother Earth,
Effortlessly showing the way to the calmer waters of life.

Tossing on the high seas,
Little vulnerable tugboat, I see your distress,
Pushing and pulling the ships to safety.
Don't burn out on your rescuing alone.

It is time to surrender.
To stop and stand still.
Choose the power of being
Over striving.
Shine Brightly.

I now realise that to achieve and sustain the ultimate life, I must continually look within and meet my needs first. Looking to others to meet our needs or ignoring or numbing our needs with quick fixes like alcohol or antidepressants can give us immediate relief but little that sustains us. These quick fixes move us away from our ultimate life because our vibration plummets, keeping us fearful, shameful and joyless. When we are feeling low, problems and grievances can seem insurmountable. Our suffering can only be healed by moving upwards, out of the vibration from where it has come.

Slowly, through venturing towards the things that make my heart sing, I have started to feel good about myself. This has allowed me to peel away patterns, behaviours and habits that do not serve me, and expose the real me. Getting to know my true self through creative play has been an extraordinary revelation. It was nearing the end of my 'gap year' that I realised I was going to consciously choose to continue this 'gap year' until the end of my life.

Living in the moment allows me to feel what I need. Unless I continually connect with the real me and put my needs first, there is no way I can offer the best me to the world. Gradually, my world is beginning to open up, with exciting new adventures, friendships and talents. I am now the happiest and most fulfilled I have been in my life. I am free to be me. I have so much more to offer my family, friends and the world.

Free to Be Me

I draw from the Cosmic Mother above and Earth Mother below.
I am deeply rooted and open to abundance of all kinds.
I am infinite potential.
I breathe in.
I breathe out through my heart, transmuting fear into love.
My heart expands
And turns the key.
I connect to my soul.
I am free to be me.

By following my joy, I am stepping away from co-dependence and towards independence and interdependence. No longer am I searching outside myself for happiness or for someone else to be responsible for my happiness. I have realised that it is only now that I truly love myself. I now put myself first, which allows me to love myself and others unconditionally. It also enables me to be loved just as I am. It is exhilarating and liberating.

It is such a new experience for me, holding the reins on my life. Gone is my family email–I now have my own email for the first time. I have also recently established my first website, **elizabethjane.com.au**. I love waking up every day, considering what I need and want, and how I can best serve others. I am excited by what lies ahead. I realise that the only person stopping me from being the leader of my life was me–not my well-meaning parents, who love me dearly and whom I love dearly, nor my teachers, my lovers, my husband or four children.

I strive for interdependence. I am totally focused on keeping my relationship with myself, loving and accepting myself just as I am, and for my future partner to keep his relationship with himself as well.

At 54 years old, I am choosing how and where I will live for the first time. I am listening to my true needs, wants and desires, and meeting them. There is so much transformation and change. Is this terrifying? Sometimes. Yet, I know it's definitely worth pushing forward into the unknown. Dear reader, I invite you to jump into the driver's seat too.

Sometimes we require baby steps. Depending on how I am feeling, a baby step forward for my day may be just nurturing myself and reassuring myself that there is no race on this journey called life and that just 'being' often brings more abundance than the 'doing.' Lashings of courage and determination are essential to keep me moving in my own forward direction. As a role model for my children, I feel quietly assured the four of them will live their lives for themselves, putting themselves first. I feel so content and peaceful knowing this. Raising my children as happy, healthy, loving and balanced young adults is my greatest achievement so far, with many more to come.

I believe that I finally have the ultimate life. As I regularly connect to my true essence through Me Time, I raise my consciousness and the consciousness of those around me. This, in turn, has connected me to those on a matching vibration, and a more abundant, peaceful, loving world has started to open up around me.

In the early hours of this morning, I saw a tiny tugboat in the harbour. Reflecting on my life, I saw that I was like the little tugboat, making the maximum effort to rescue those that I loved, giving my power away but that was also disempowering for my loved ones. We were all, in effect, on the sinking boat together.

However, as I step into my authentic self, I feel that I have become the powerful lighthouse, with ease and grace, guiding by beaming my light across the obstacles and perils. I am standing tall, living by example, showing and sharing my knowledge and wisdom to those who are ready. I truly hope that you will choose to beam your light, take this knowledge for yourself and share it with others. It's time to free ourselves and embrace a happy and healthy life, lived from the heart.

Into the Light

Such joy, such bliss.
My heart blossoms.
1000 lotus petals open
Showering me with crystal rain.
I am alive,
Awake from this dream.

Moonlight Magic

Almighty Akasha,
Universal Lord,
Holding us tight in place each night,
The speckle of stars sparkle
As the moon masters the dark sky,
Orchestrating its light,
Serenaded by the clouds.
The waves dance,
Kissing the shore.
Birds faintly whistle
Their delight
Hidden by the night.
Nature is awake.
Humanity in slumber.

About the Author

Elizabeth Jane is a painter, poet, writer and author. She openly shares her transformational journey through a difficult and painful divorce encouraging others to embark on their own uplifting journey to find inner happiness and become the master of their mind and the leader of their life.

Born in Melbourne, Australia and now living in Sydney, New South Wales, Elizabeth has four adult children and a deep passion for creativity and uplifting those around her. She graduated with a Bachelor of Commerce and later completed a Diploma in Education, initially working as an accountant and then moving into primary school teaching. More recently, Elizabeth has found her true joy in creative expression, firmly believing that creative therapy is the key to discovering one's true potential and happiness. Today she is an active mentor and spokesperson who focuses on writing, keynote speaking, yoga and meditation, painting, travelling and spending time with her family.

An eternal optimist, Elizabeth hopes to inspire others to unlock their joy and live their best life through her insights, learnings, tools and encouragement.

How to Purchase Elizabeth's Art

Elizabeth's current art collection, including the artworks in this book, can be purchased via her website at: www.elizabethjane.com.au

Appendix 1

Transformational tools

To break old patterns, habits and behaviours that no longer serve you, I invite you to adhere to this program for at least forty days. Maybe partner with a good friend or colleague to work through the steps. You will likely want to continue this program longer, as the benefits to your overall sense of wellbeing will speak for themselves. Each day:

- exercise gratitude: journal one thing that is thriving in your life;
- be creative: choose one that brings you joy;
- remember your boundaries: be mindful and choose not to overstep them;
- be open: say 'yes' to opportunities that make your heart sing;
- breathe deeply: practise deep breathing techniques in times of stress;
- use the forgiveness mantra: chant for yourself or someone who is challenging you;
- make alone time: allocate ten minutes to meditate or to be with nature;
- be in the now: tune in consciously to be in the present moment and aware of all your senses; and
- practise self-love: choose one practice from Appendix 2.

Appendix 2

Self-love practices

Practising self-love can involve anything that is nourishing for you and brings you joy. I have realised over the last three years that taking care of myself is taking care of others. Unless I can put myself first, I am not in a position to care for others effectively.

Below is my Self-Love Practices List. I am sure you can add your own flavour to this list. I was surprised at how much more peaceful, joyous and fun life became after a few months of implementing these practices. Remember, be spontaneous and follow your heart, not your head.

1. Experiment with a new creative hobby that interests you.
2. Buy yourself fresh flowers.
3. Take a bubble bath.
4. Give yourself a massage with your favourite essential oils.
5. Spend time with nature by taking a short walk or hike, or camp out.
6. Write in your gratitude diary daily.
7. Buy something for yourself without guilt.
8. Commit to self-care of your body, including your nails and hair.
9. Contact a loved one to tell them, 'I love you.'
10. Host a spontaneous party where each guest brings a special friend and a small plate of food to share.
11. Cuddle up to a special loved one, pets included.
12. Watch your favourite movie.
13. Turn off your alarm and sleep in on the weekend.
14. Take up an activity that you enjoyed as a child.
15. Affirm to yourself each morning, 'I am beautiful, I am bountiful, I am more than enough.'

16. Declutter your home and office; surround yourself with things that are really special to you.
17. Take time to rest and relax without guilt.
18. Meditate or breathe deeply for at least five minutes per day.
19. Read a book that interests you.
20. Say 'no' to uninspiring and self-limiting choices.
21. Say 'yes' to opportunities and choices that open your heart.
22. Stock your kitchen with healthy food that you love.
23. List at least ten things you love about yourself and put it on the fridge door or bathroom mirror.
24. Give and receive compliments with a smile.
25. Sweat, move and shake your body daily to de-stress.
26. Book an appointment with a counsellor or doctor.
27. Journal and express your feelings.
28. Be in the moment with one or more of your senses.
29. Wear your favourite outfit just because you can.
30. Laugh out loud for no reason at all.

Appendix 3

About Kundalini

When I first heard the word *Kundalini*, I thought it was a type of pasta! Little did I know that it was to be my saving grace. I have been practising Kundalini for three years now and, without a doubt, it has helped me establish an aligned relationship between my body, mind and soul.

Kundalini is often referred to as the self-awareness yoga. The practice involves a combination of powerful breathing techniques, postures, mantras and meditation. With eyes closed and a focus on your breath, the practice allows you to go deep within yourself. The aim of Kundalini is to release stress in the system, enabling you to live in your full vitality. Unreleased stress in the body often manifests into physical, nutritional or emotional imbalances, resulting in illness or a lack of energy.

My favourite Kundalini teacher, Robbie Chapman, who has her own practice, Kundalini Healing, in the Eastern Suburbs of Sydney, believes that 'we owe it to ourselves and those around us to be open to change, let go of old patterns and live fully in the present.'

Please feel free to visit the website of the global Kundalini foundation 3HO to find a studio near you or an online class at: www.3ho.org.

Appendix 4

Further reading

Below is a list of books that I have found useful and recommend for further reading as these titles expand on many of the ideas in this book.

By Akal Pritam
Self-Love: Finding Peace and Happiness

By Amy Morin
13 Things Mentally Strong People Don't Do

By Anders Olsson
Conscious Breathing

By Anthony William
Medical Medium Liver Rescue: Answers to Eczema, Psoriasis, Diabetes, Strep, Acne, Gout, Bloating, Gallstones, Adrenal Stress, Fatigue, Fatty Liver, Weight Issues, SIBO & Autoimmune Disease

By Cassie Mendoza-Jones
You Are Enough: How To Elevate Your Thoughts, Align Your Energy & Get Out of the Comparison Trap

By Dr Charles Whitfield
Healing the Child Within: Discovery and Recovery for Adult Children of Dysfunctional Families

By Charles L. Whitfield, M.D.
Boundaries and Relationships: Knowing, Protecting and Enjoying the Self

By Cristien Storm
Empowered Boundaries: Speaking Truth, Setting Boundaries, and Inspiring Social Change

By Dannielle Miller, B. Ed
The Butterfly Effect: A Positive New Approach to Raising Happy, Confident Teen Girls

By Deepak Chopra and Menas C. Kafatos
You Are the Universe: Discovering Your Cosmic Self and Why It Matters

By Dharm Khalsa and Karena Virginia
Essential Kundalini Yoga: An Invitation to Radiant Health, Unconditional Love and the Awakening of Your Energetic Potential

By Eckhart Tolle
The Power of Now, A Guide to Spiritual Enlightenment
The New Earth, Create a Better Life

By Gabrielle Bernstein
Judgement Detox

By Dr Gillian McKeith
Food Bible: How to Use Food to Cure What Ails You
You Are What You Eat: The Plan That Will Change Your Life

By GuruMeher Khalsa
Senses of the Soul: Emotional Therapy for Strength, Healing and Guidance

By Joe Vitale and Dr Ihaleakakala Hew Len
Zero Limits: The Secret Hawaiian System for Wealth, Health, Peace and More

By Julia Cameron
The Artist's Way

By Kulreet Chaudhary, M.D.
Sound Medicine: How to Use the Ancient Science of Sound to Heal the Body and Mind

By Lucia Capacchione
Recovery of Your Inner Child

By Melody Beattie
The New Codependency
Beyond Codependency
Codependent No More
The Language of Letting Go

By Michael A. Singer
The Untethered Soul: The Journey Beyond Yourself

By Nathaniel Branden
The Psychology of Self-Esteem
How to Raise Your Self-Esteem
The Six Pillars of Self-Esteem

By Osho
The Power of Love

By Paramahansa Yogananda
Autobiography of a Yogi

By Pia Mellody
Facing Codependence (with Andrea Wells Miller and J. Keith Miller)
The Intimacy Factor: The Ground Rules for Overcoming the Obstacles to Truth, Respect, and Lasting Love (with Lawrence S. Freundlich)

By Shakti Durga
Empowering Relationships: Practical, Spiritual Approaches to Create Great Relationships

By Dr Vasant Lad
Ayurveda: The Science of Self-Healing

By Viktor E. Frankl
Man's Search for Meaning

By Dr Wayne W. Dyer
Your Erroneous Zones: Step-by-Step Advice for Escaping the Trap of Negative Thinking and Taking Control of Your Life
Inspiration: Your Ultimate Calling
Excuses Begone! How to Change Lifelong Self-Defeating Thinking Habits
I Can See Clearly Now
Change Your Thoughts, Change Your Life: Living the Wisdom of the Tao
There is a Spiritual Solution to Every Problem
The Shift: Taking your Life from Ambition to Meaning
What Do You Really Want For Your Children?
101 Ways to Transform Your Life

Appendix 5
Resources

3ho.org
Kundalini Foundation and Yoga Classes:
3HO Foundation

anjaniamriit.com
Coach for heart-driven entrepreneurs and visionaries

antoinettesampson.com
Inner peace activist, author and teacher

cyndiart.com
Painting classes in Sydney's Eastern Suburbs
The Rogoff Art School

jennynurick.com
Psychotherapist, counsellor and energetic healer

kundalinihealing.com.au
Kundalini Yoga and Kinesiology

narayanipeedam.org
Words of wisdom from Sri Narayani Peedam

oneworldayurveda.com
Oneworld Ayurveda is Southeast Asia's leading Ayurvedic centre offering genuine Panchakarma detox programs

raise.org.au
Raise Foundation: a powerful youth mentoring movement creating thriving communities across Australia

srinarayaniholisticcentre.com
Sri Narayani Holistic Centre Health Spa

sydneyyogacollective.com
Sydney Yoga Collective

YouTube
Sri Narayani Peedam, Sripuram Golden Temple–About Amma

A selection of crisis and support services in Australia:

Lifeline
lifeline.org.au
13 11 14

Kids Helpline
kidshelpline.com.au
1800 55 1800

Black Dog Institute
blackdoginstitute.org.au
02 9382 4530

Beyond Blue
beyondblue.org.au
1300 22 46 36

Headspace
headspace.com
1800 650 890

Note-taking page for self-reflection

www.ingramcontent.com/pod-product-compliance
Ingram Content Group UK Ltd.
Pitfield, Milton Keynes, MK11 3LW, UK
UKHW062141200426
470212UK00001B/1

9781923250048